Sunset COTTAGE
CABIN & VACATION
home plans

SUNSET BOOKS

VICE PRESIDENT, GENERAL MANAGER
  Richard A. Smeby
VICE PRESIDENT, EDITORIAL DIRECTOR
  Bob Doyle
DIRECTOR OF OPERATIONS
  Rosann Sutherland
MARKETING MANAGER
  Linda Barker
ART DIRECTOR
  Vasken Guiragossian
SPECIAL SALES
  Brad Moses

DEVELOPMENTAL EDITOR
  Carrie Dodson Davis
PRODUCTION SPECIALIST
  Linda M. Bouchard

10 9 8 7 6 5 4 3 2 1
First Printing March 2007

ISBN-13: 978-0-376-01116-9
ISBN-10: 0-376-01116-5

Library of Congress Control Number:
2006935331. Printed in the United
States of America.

For additional copies of *Cottage, Cabin
& Vacation Home Plans* or any other Sunset
book, visit us at www.sunsetbooks.com
or call 1-800-526-5111.

COVER
Plan #032D-0040 (page 247)
Designed by DrummondDesigns.com.

table of contents

Plan #588-007D-0060. For more information please see page 11.

Plan #588-022D-0007. For more information please see page 123.

Plan #588-016D-0062. For more information please see page 122.

Plan #588-022D-0018. For more information please see page 142 .

about this book

Are you in need of a getaway? A place to get away from the stress of daily life. A place surrounded by beautiful scenery with gorgeous views. A place where your family and friends will come to gather together to make lifetime memories.

Where you go to get away from life is just as important as where you live the rest of the year. Whether you're looking for a weekend retreat or an extended vacation home, your getaway spot will be even more magical if it has all the comforts of home. Make your dream escape a reality with our spectacular home plans.

Cottage, Cabin and Vacation Home Plans will inspire you with over 300 home plans designed for comfort and function. Our collection includes something for everyone, including small hunting cabins, cozy lodge retreats, beach cottages, and tranquil lake resorts. Most of our homes include all the necessities for full-time living making them ideal for starter homes or retirement living.

The floor plans are designed for ease of living, eliminating the stress of everyday life. Convenience is key when you need to relax.

Our plans also include abundant windows that let the sunshine in and porches and decks providing outdoor living, welcoming the refreshing breeze.

Get ready to start the journey of finding your dream vacation home. With the breadth of styles included in this book, we're sure there is an enchanting home just for you.

what is the right plan for you?

Many of the homes you see may appear to be just what you're looking for. But are they? One way to find out is to carefully analyze what you want in a home. This is an important first step we'll show you how to take.

For most people, budget is the most critical element in narrowing the choices. Generally, the size of the home, or, specifically, the square footage of living area is the most important criteria in establishing the cost of a new home.

Your next task is to consider the style of home you want. Should it be traditional, contemporary, one-story or two-story? If yours is an infill lot in an existing neighborhood, is the design you like compatible with the existing residential architecture? If not, will the subdivision permit you to build the design of your choice?

And what about the site itself? What will it allow you to do and what won't it allow you to do?

Site topography is the first consideration in floor plan development. Slopes, both gentle and steep, will affect the home design you select. If you want a multi-level home with a walk-out basement that appears to be a single-story residence from the street, you need a lot that slopes from front to back. And what about the garage? Do you prefer access at street level or a lower level?

Next, there is the issue of orientation, that is, the direction in which you want the house to face. Considering the north-south or east-west orientation of the site itself, will the plan you choose allow you to enjoy sweeping views from the living room? Does the design have a lot of glass on the south side that will permit you to take advantage of the sun's warmth in winter?

Now for the tough part; figuring out what you want inside the house to satisfy your needs and lifestyle. To a large extent, that may depend on where you are in life – just starting out, whether you have toddlers or teenagers, whether you're an "empty-nester," or retired.

Next, think about the components of the home. Do you want, or need, both a living room and family room or would just one large great room suffice? Do you want, or need, both a breakfast room and a formal dining room? How many bedrooms, full baths and half baths do you need? How much storage? And what about space for working from home, hobbies or a workshop?

When you've completed your wish list, think about how you want your home to function. In architectural terms, think about spatial relationships and circulation, or in other words, the relationship of each of the components to one another.

For example, to deliver groceries conveniently, the kitchen should be directly accessible from the garage. To serve meals efficiently, the dining area should be adjacent to the kitchen. The same principle applies to other areas and components of the home. Consider the flow from entry foyer to living, sleeping, and food preparation areas.

> **Experts in the field suggest that the best way to determine your needs is to begin by listing everything you like or dislike about your current home.**

As you study your favorite home plan, ask yourself if it's possible to close off certain spaces to eliminate noise from encroaching upon others. For instance, if you enjoy listening to music, you don't want it drowned out by a droning dishwasher or blaring TV being watched by another member of the family nearby. Similarly, sleeping areas and bathrooms should be remote from living areas. After you've come to terms with the types and relationship of rooms you want in your dream home, you can then concentrate on the size and features you want for each of those spaces.

If cooking is a hobby and you entertain frequently, you might want a large gourmet kitchen or even the ever-so-popular outdoor kitchen. If you like openness and a laid-back environment, you might want a large family room with picture windows, a fireplace, vaulted ceiling, and exposed wood beams. A central living area directly accessible to an outdoor deck or patio is the ultimate in casual, relaxed style.

Deciding what you want in your dream home, where you want it, and how you want it to look is thought provoking and time consuming, but careful planning and thought will have a great return on investment when it comes to you and your family's happiness.

making changes to your plan

We understand that it is difficult to find blueprints for a home that will meet all your needs. That is why HDA, Inc. (Home Design Alternatives) is pleased to offer home plan modification services.

typical home plan modifications include:

- Changing foundation type
- Adding square footage to a plan
- Changing the entry into a garage
- Changing a two-car garage to a three-car garage or making a garage larger
- Redesigning kitchen, baths, and bedrooms
- Changing exterior elevations
- Or most other home plan modifications you may desire!

some home plan modifications we cannot make include:

- Reversing the plans
- Adapting/engineering plans to meet your local building codes
- Combining parts of two different plans (due to copyright laws)

our plan modification service is easy to use. simply:

1. Decide on the modifications you want. For the most accurate quote, be as detailed as possible and refer to rooms in the same manner as the floor plan (i.e. if the floor plan refers to a "den", then use "den" in your description). Including a sketch of the modified floor plan is always helpful.

2. Request from our customer service department a modification request form by calling 1-800-367-7667 and then fill it out with your requests and return by fax, email or mail.

3. Within two business days, you will receive your quote. Quotes do not include the cost of the reproducible masters required for our designer to legally make changes.

4. Call to accept the quote and purchase the reproducible masters. For example, if your quote is $850 and the reproducible masters for your plan are $800, your order total will be $1650 plus two shipping and handling charges (one to ship the reproducible masters to our designer and one to ship the modified plans to you).

5. Our designer will send you up to three drafts to verify your initial changes. Extra costs apply after the third draft. If additional changes are made that alter the original request, extra charges may be incurred.

6. Once you approve a draft with the final changes, we then make the changes to the reproducible masters by adding additional sheets. The original reproducible masters (with no changes) plus your new changed sheets will be shipped to you.

other important information:

- Plans cannot be redrawn in reverse format. All modifications will be made to match the reproducible master's original layout. Once you receive the plans, you can make reverse copies at your local blueprint shop.
- Our staff designer will provide the first draft for your review within 4 weeks (plus shipping time) of receiving your order.
- You will receive up to three drafts to review before your original changes are modified. The first draft will totally encompass all modifications based on your original request. Additional changes not included in your original request will be charged separately at an hourly rate of $75 or a flat quoted rate.
- Modifications will be drawn on a separate sheet with the changes shown and a note to see the main sheet for details. For example, a floor plan sheet from the original set (i.e. Sheet 3) would be followed by a new floor plan sheet with changes (i.e. Sheet A-3).
- Plans are drawn to meet national building codes. Modifications will not be drawn to any particular state or county codes, thus we cannot guarantee that the revisions will meet your local building codes. You may be required to have a local architect or designer review the plans in order to have them comply with your state or county building codes.
- Time and cost estimates are good for 90 calendar days.
- All modification requests need to be submitted in writing. Verbal requests will not be accepted.

---

2 easy steps for FAST service

1. Visit www.houseplansandmore.com to download the modification request form.

2. E-mail the completed form to customize@hdainc.com or fax to 913-856-7751.

If you are not able to access the internet, please call 1-800-367-7667 (Monday-Friday, 8am-5pm CST).

plan #588-062D-0048

plan information

total living area:	1,543
bedrooms:	3
baths:	2
foundation type:	
crawl space	

special features

- energy efficient home with 2" x 6" exterior walls
- enormous sundeck makes this a popular vacation style
- a woodstove warms the vaulted living and dining rooms
- a vaulted kitchen has a prep island and breakfast bar
- second floor vaulted master bedroom has a private bath and walk-in closet

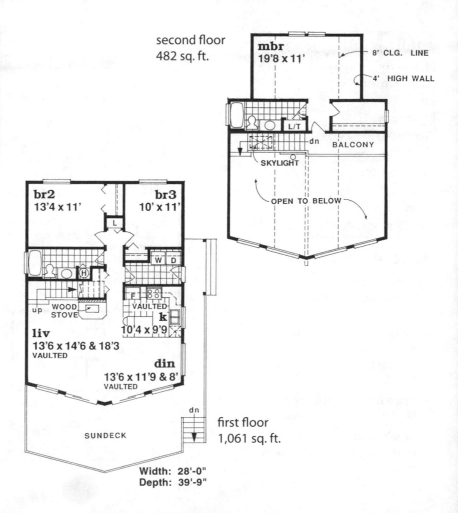

second floor
482 sq. ft.

mbr
19'8 x 11'

8' CLG. LINE

4' HIGH WALL

L/T

dn   BALCONY

SKYLIGHT

OPEN TO BELOW

br2
13'4 x 11'

br3
10' x 11'

L

W   D

up   WOOD STOVE

F   VAULTED

k
10'4 x 9'9

liv
13'6 x 14'6 & 18'3
VAULTED

din
13'6 x 11'9 & 8'
VAULTED

dn

first floor
1,061 sq. ft.

SUNDECK

Width: 28'-0"
Depth: 39'-9"

plan information

total living area:	1,525
bedrooms:	3
baths:	2
garage:	2-car

foundation types:
- basement
- walk-out basement
- crawl space
- slab

please specify when ordering

special features

- corner fireplace is highlighted in the great room
- unique glass block window over the whirlpool tub in the master bath brightens the interior
- open bar overlooks both the kitchen and great room
- breakfast room leads to an outdoor grilling and covered porch

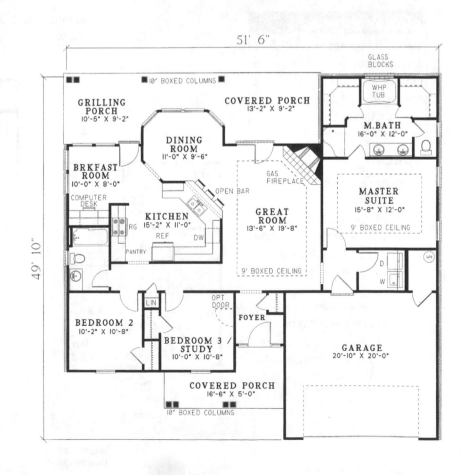

plan information

total living area:	1,660
bedrooms:	3
baths:	3
foundation types:	

partial basement/crawl
space standard
slab

special features

- energy efficient home with 2" x 6" exterior walls
- convenient gear and equipment room
- spacious living and dining rooms look even larger with the openness of the foyer and kitchen
- large wrap-around deck is a great plus for outdoor living
- broad balcony overlooks living and dining rooms

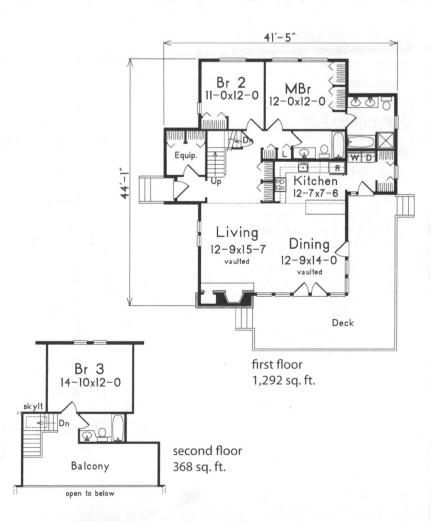

first floor
1,292 sq. ft.

second floor
368 sq. ft.

plan information

total living area:	1,452
bedrooms:	4
baths:	2
foundation type:	
basement	

special features

- large living room features a cozy corner fireplace, bayed dining area and access from the entry with guest closet
- forward master bedroom enjoys having its own bath and linen closet
- three additional bedrooms share a bath with a double-bowl vanity

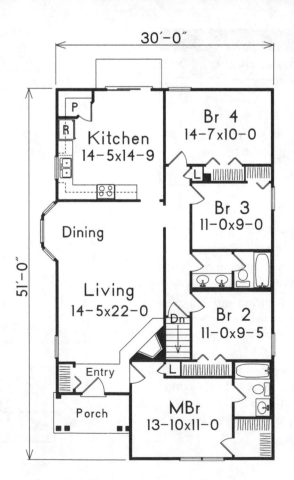

order 1-800-367-7667

plan information

total living area:	864
bedrooms:	2
baths:	1
foundation types:	
crawl space standard	
basement	
slab	

special features

- an L-shaped kitchen with convenient pantry is adjacent to the dining area
- easy access to laundry area, linen closet and storage closet
- both bedrooms include ample closet space

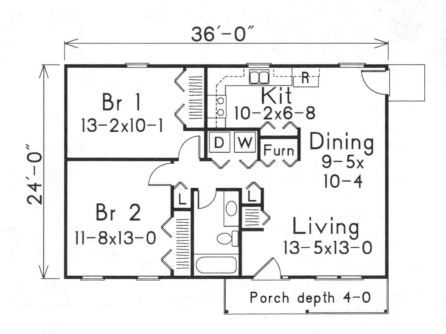

order 1-800-367-7667

plan information

total living area:	1,833
bedrooms:	3
baths:	2 1/2
garage:	2-car detached side entry
foundation types:	crawl space standard slab

special features

- large master bedroom includes a spacious bath with garden tub, separate shower and large walk-in closet
- the spacious dining area is brightened by large windows and patio access
- detached two-car garage with walkway leading to house adds charm to this country home

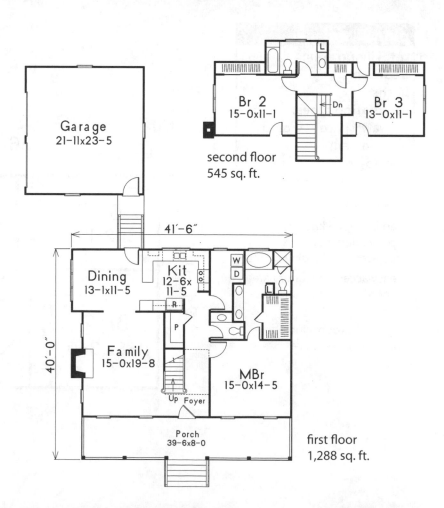

Garage
21-11x23-5

Br 2
15-0x11-1

Br 3
13-0x11-1

Dn

second floor
545 sq. ft.

41'-6"

Dining
13-1x11-5

Kit
12-6x
11-5

W D

Family
15-0x19-8

40'-0"

R

P

MBr
15-0x14-5

Up Foyer

Porch
39-6x8-0

first floor
1,288 sq. ft.

order 1-800-367-7667

plan information

total living area:	1,268
bedrooms:	3
baths:	2
garage:	2-car
foundation types:	
basement standard	
crawl space	
slab	

special features

- multiple gables, large porch and arched windows create a classy exterior
- innovative design provides openness in the great room, kitchen and breakfast room
- secondary bedrooms have private hall with bath

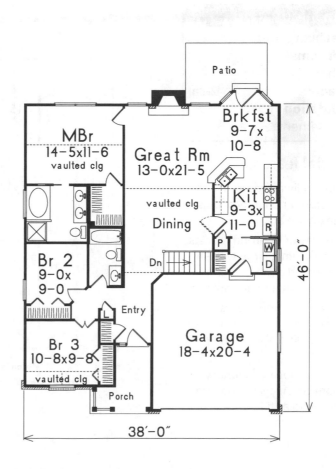

plan #588-004D-0002

price code C

plan information

total living area:	1,823
bedrooms:	3
baths:	2
garage:	2-car
foundation type:	
basement	

special features

- vaulted living room is spacious and easily accesses the dining area
- the master bedroom boasts a tray ceiling, large walk-in closet and a private bath with a corner whirlpool tub
- cheerful dining area is convenient to the U-shaped kitchen and also enjoys patio access
- centrally located laundry room connects the garage to the living areas

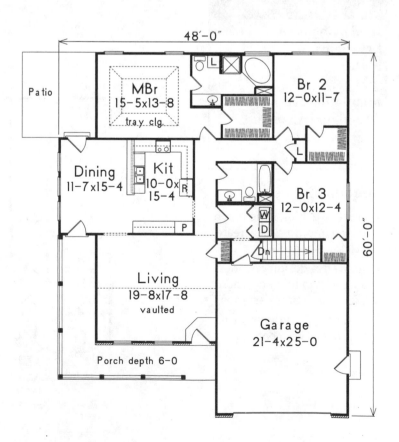

plan information

total living area:	972
bedrooms:	2
baths:	1
foundation type:	
basement	

special features

- energy efficient home with 2" x 6" exterior walls
- spacious dining area overlooks into kitchen
- two bedrooms separated by a large shared bath
- convenient laundry closet
- cheerful bay window in living area

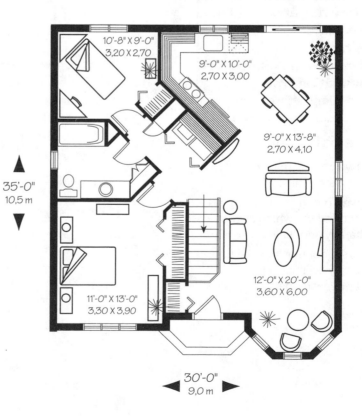

10'-8" X 9'-0"
3,20 X 2,70

9'-0" X 10'-0"
2,70 X 3,00

9'-0" X 13'-8"
2,70 X 4,10

35'-0"
10,5 m

12'-0" X 20'-0"
3,60 X 6,00

11'-0" X 13'-0"
3,30 X 3,90

30'-0"
9,0 m

plan information

total living area:	1,491
bedrooms:	3
baths:	2 1/2
garage:	2-car drive under
foundation type:	
walk-out basement	

special features

- two-story family room has a vaulted ceiling
- well-organized kitchen has a serving bar which overlooks family and dining rooms
- first floor master suite has a tray ceiling, walk-in closet and master bath

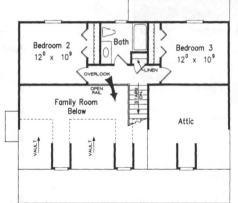

second floor
430 sq. ft.

first floor
1,061 sq. ft.

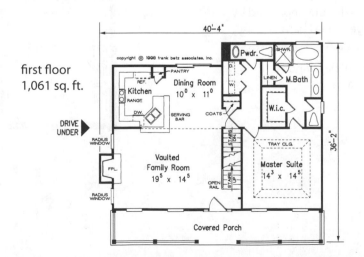

plan information

total living area:	1,711
bedrooms:	2
baths:	2 1/2
foundation type:	
basement	

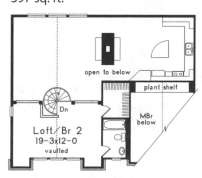

rear view

special features

- entry leads to a vaulted great room with exposed beams, two-story window wall, fireplace, wet bar and balcony
- bayed breakfast room shares the fireplace and joins a sun-drenched kitchen and deck
- vaulted first floor master bedroom features a double-door entry, two closets and bookshelves
- spiral stairs and a balcony dramatize the loft that doubles as a spacious second bedroom

second floor
397 sq. ft.

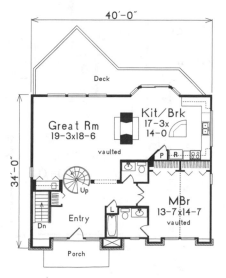

first floor
1,314 sq. ft.

plan information

total living area:	1,550
bedrooms:	3
baths:	2
garage:	2-car
foundation type:	
slab	

special features

- alcove in the family room can be used as a cozy corner fireplace or as a media center
- master bedroom features a large walk-in closet, skylight and separate tub and shower
- convenient laundry closet
- kitchen with pantry and breakfast bar connects to the family room
- family room and master bedroom access the covered patio

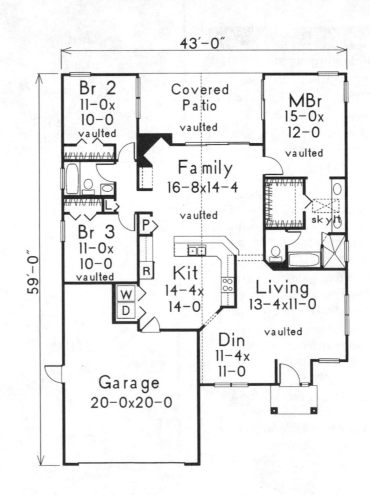

order 1-800-367-7667

plan information

total living area:	1,200
bedrooms:	3
baths:	1 1/2
foundation types:	
crawl space standard slab	

special features

- ornate ranch-style railing enhances exterior while the stone fireplace provides a visual anchor
- spectacular living room features an inviting fireplace and adjoins a charming kitchen with dining area
- two second floor bedrooms share a full bath

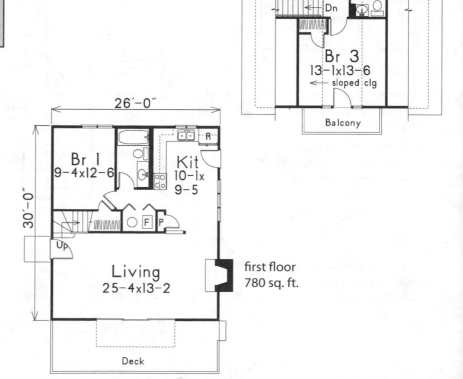

second floor
420 sq. ft.

Br 2
13-1x10-1

Dn

Br 3
13-1x13-6
← sloped clg

Balcony

26'-0"

30'-0"

Br 1
9-4x12-6

Kit
10-1x
9-5

Up

Living
25-4x13-2

first floor
780 sq. ft.

Deck

order 1-800-367-7667

plan information

total living area:	1,630
bedrooms:	3
baths:	2
garage:	2-car
foundation type:	
basement	

special features

- crisp facade and full windows front and back offer open viewing
- wrap-around rear deck is accessible from the breakfast room, dining room and master bedroom
- vaulted ceilings top the living room and master bedroom
- sitting area and large walk-in closet complement the master bedroom

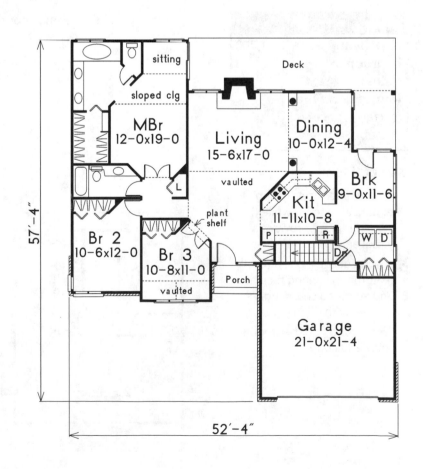

plan #588-016D-0032

price code A

special features

- energy efficient home with 2" x 6" exterior walls
- great room includes an oversized stone fireplace for cozy gatherings
- second floor includes den/studio/bedroom #3 offering flexibility

second floor
544 sq. ft.

first floor
952 sq. ft.

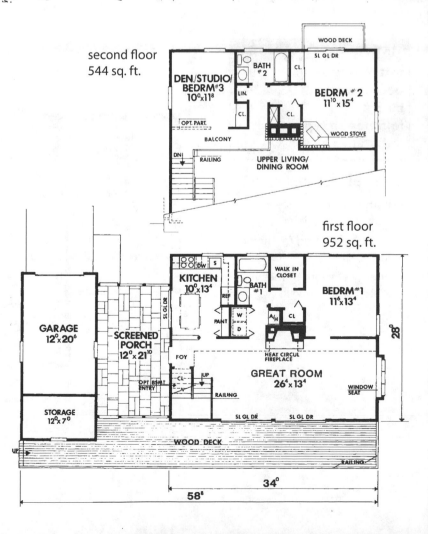

plan information

total living area:	920
bedrooms:	2
baths:	1
foundation type:	
basement	

special features

- bath has extra space for a washer and dryer
- plenty of seating for dining at the kitchen counter
- energy efficient home with 2" x 6" exterior walls

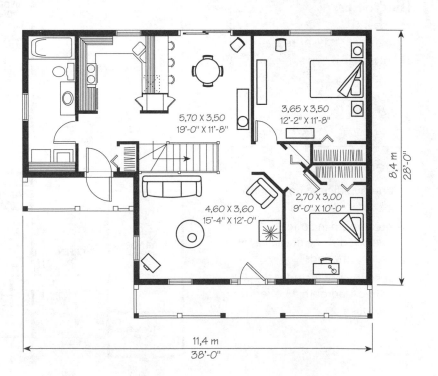

plan information

total living area:	1,737
bedrooms:	3
baths:	2 1/2

foundation types:
  slab
  crawl space
please specify when ordering

special features

- the U-shaped kitchen, sunny bayed breakfast room and living area become one large gathering area
- living area has a sloped ceiling and a balcony overlook from the second floor
- second floor includes lots of storage area

second floor
499 sq. ft.

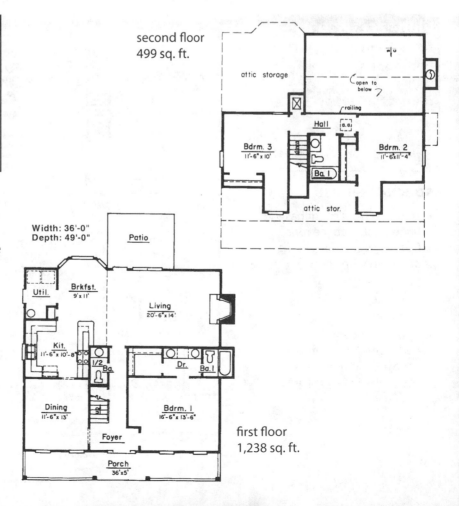

Width: 36'-0"
Depth: 49'-0"

first floor
1,238 sq. ft.

plan information

total living area:	1,455
bedrooms:	2
baths:	2
foundation types:	
slab	
crawl space	
please specify when ordering	

special features

- spacious mud room has a large pantry, space for a freezer, sink/counter area and bath with shower
- bedroom #2 can easily be converted to a study or office area
- optional second floor bedroom and playroom have an additional 744 square feet of living area

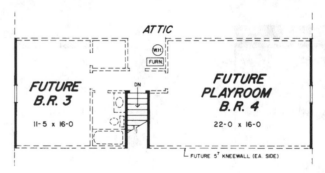

optional second floor

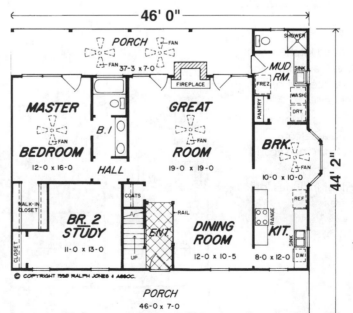

first floor
1,455 sq. ft.

plan #588-055D-0100

plan information

total living area:	1,294
bedrooms:	2
baths:	2
garage:	2-car

foundation types:
  crawl space
  slab
please specify when ordering

special features

- second floor bedroom #2/loft has its own bath and a vaulted ceiling overlooking to the great room below

- great room has a cozy fireplace and accesses both the front and the rear of the home

- laundry area on the first floor is convenient to the kitchen

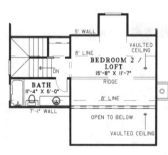

second floor
322 sq. ft.

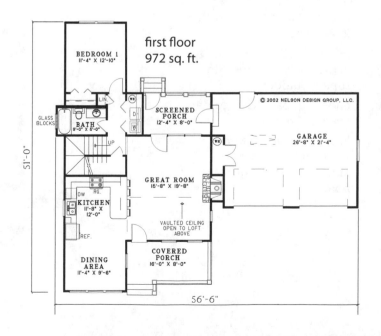

first floor
972 sq. ft.

© 2002 Nelson Design Group, LLC.

plan #588-032D-0050

price code AAA

plan information

total living area:	840
bedrooms:	1
baths:	1
foundation type:	
walk-out basement	

special features

- energy efficient home with 2" x 6" exterior walls
- prominent gazebo located in the rear of the home for superb outdoor living
- enormous bath has a corner oversized tub
- lots of windows create a cheerful and sunny atmosphere throughout this home

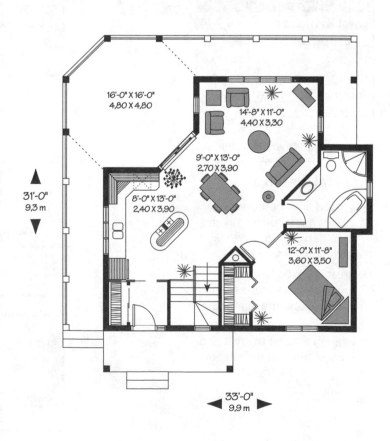

16'-0" X 16'-0"
4,80 X 4,80

14'-8" X 11'-0"
4,40 X 3,30

9'-0" X 13'-0"
2,70 X 3,90

8'-0" X 13'-0"
2,40 X 3,90

12'-0" X 11'-8"
3,60 X 3,50

31'-0"
9,3 m

33'-0"
9,9 m

plan #588-022D-0020   price code AA

plan information

total living area:	988
bedrooms:	2
baths:	1
garage:	2-car
foundation type:	
basement	

special features

- great room features a corner fireplace
- vaulted ceiling and corner windows add space and light in great room
- eat-in kitchen with vaulted ceiling accesses deck for outdoor living
- master bedroom features separate vanities and private access to the bath

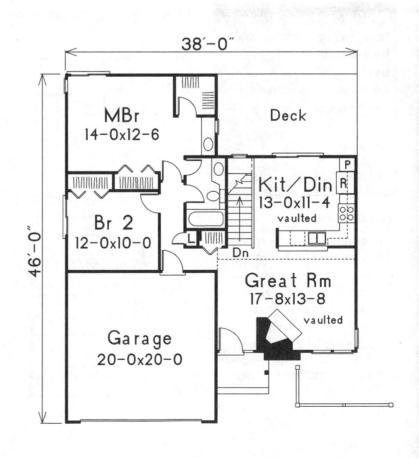

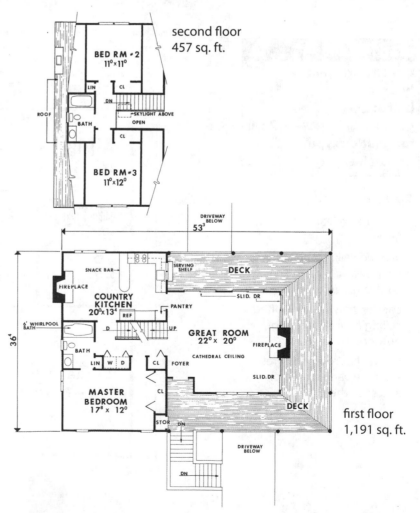

second floor
457 sq. ft.

BED RM #2
11⁰ x 11⁰

BED RM #3
11⁰ x 12⁰

first floor
1,191 sq. ft.

plan information

total living area: 1,648
bedrooms: 3
baths: 2
garage: 2-car drive under
foundation types:
  basement
  crawl space
  slab
please specify when ordering

special features

- enormous country kitchen has fireplace and a snack bar
- four sets of sliding glass doors fill this home full of light and make the deck convenient from any room
- secondary bedrooms are both located on the second floor along with a full bath

plan #588-007D-0037

plan information

total living area:	1,403
bedrooms:	3
baths:	2
garage:	2-car drive under
foundation type:	
	basement

special features

- impressive living areas for a modest-sized home
- special master/hall bath has linen storage, step-up tub and lots of window light
- spacious closets everywhere you look

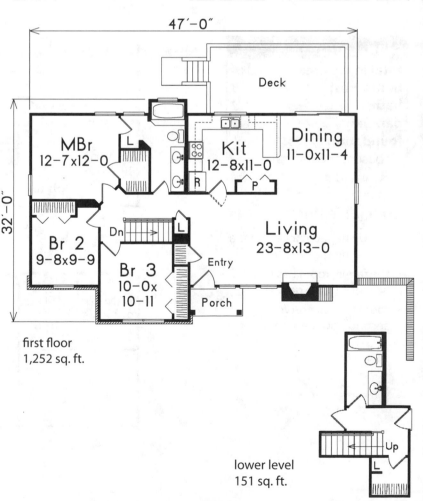

first floor
1,252 sq. ft.

lower level
151 sq. ft.

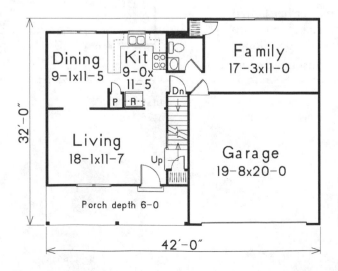

plan information

total living area:	1,314
bedrooms:	3
baths:	1 1/2
garage:	2-car
foundation types:	
basement standard	
crawl space	

special features

- the U-shaped kitchen joins a cozy dining area
- the family room has direct access into the garage
- roomy closets serve the second floor bedrooms

Br 2
13-1x10-1

Dn

MBr
11-2x12-7

Br 3
9-10x9-3

second floor
552 sq. ft.

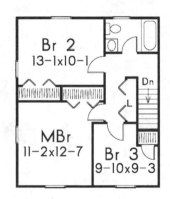

Dining
9-1x11-5

Kit
9-0x
11-5

Family
17-3x11-0

P   R

Dn

32'-0"

Living
18-1x11-7

Up

Garage
19-8x20-0

Porch depth 6-0

42'-0"

first floor
762 sq. ft.

plan #588-008D-0140

plan information

total living area:	1,391
bedrooms:	2
baths:	1
foundation types:	
pier standard	
crawl space	

special features

- large living room with masonry fireplace features a soaring vaulted ceiling

- a spiral staircase in the hall leads to a huge loft area overlooking the living room below

- two first floor bedrooms share a full bath

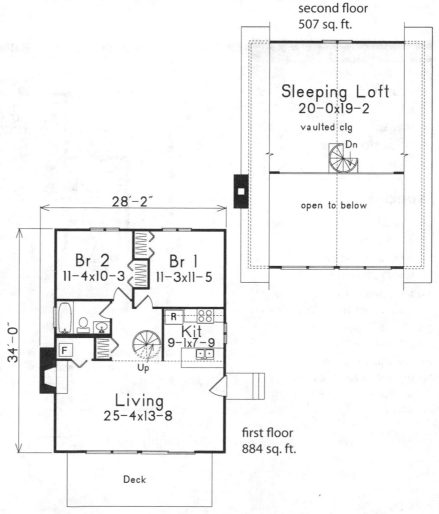

second floor
507 sq. ft.

Sleeping Loft
20-0x19-2
vaulted clg

Dn

open to below

28'-2"

34'-0"

Br 2
11-4x10-3

Br 1
11-3x11-5

Kit
9-1x7-9

Up

Living
25-4x13-8

first floor
884 sq. ft.

Deck

plan information

total living area:	1,295
bedrooms:	2
baths:	2
garage:	2-car
foundation type:	
basement	

special features

- energy efficient home with 2" x 6" exterior walls
- wrap-around porch is a lovely place for dining
- a fireplace gives a stunning focal point to the great room that is heightened with a sloped ceiling
- the master suite is full of luxurious touches such as a walk-in closet and a lush private bath

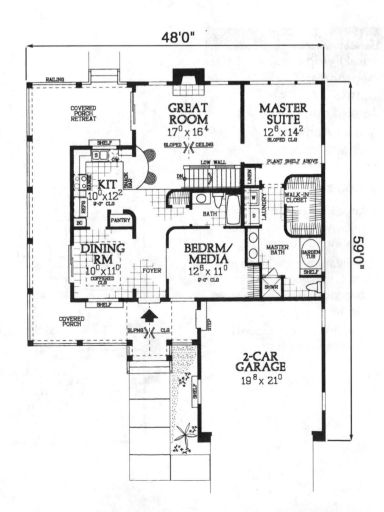

plan #588-007D-0109

price code AAA

plan information

total living area:	888
bedrooms:	2
baths:	1
garage:	1-car
foundation type:	
basement	

special features

- home features an eye-catching exterior and has a spacious porch
- the breakfast room with bay window is open to the living room and adjoins the kitchen with pass-through snack bar
- the bedrooms are quite roomy and feature walk-in closets
- the master bedroom has a double-door entry and access to the rear patio

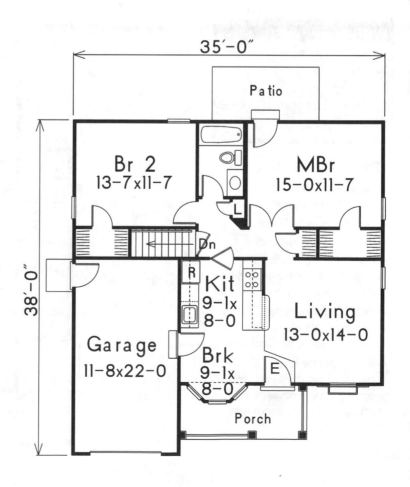

order 1-800-367-7667

plan information

total living area:	950
bedrooms:	2
baths:	1
foundation type:	
crawl space	

special features

- energy efficient home with 2" x 6" exterior walls
- two porches provide relaxing atmospheres
- the combined living and dining areas are warmed by a large hearth fireplace
- wrap-around kitchen offers a pantry, laundry area and plant window beyond sink
- a spectacular loft overlooking the living and dining areas provides an additional 270 square feet of living area

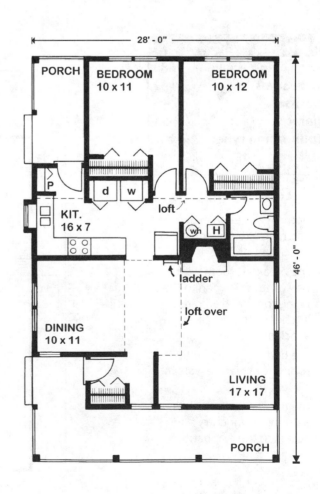

plan #588-008D-0153

order 1-800-367-7667

plan information

total living area:	792
bedrooms:	2
baths:	1
foundation types:	
crawl space standard	
slab	

special features

- attractive exterior features wood posts and beams, wrap-around deck with railing and glass sliding doors with transoms
- kitchen, living and dining areas enjoy sloped ceilings, a cozy fireplace and views over the deck
- two bedrooms share a bath just off the hall

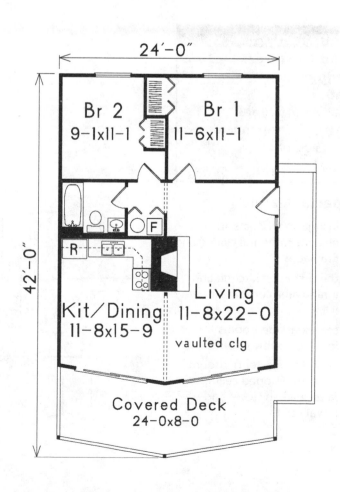

24'-0"

42'-0"

Br 2
9-1x11-1

Br 1
11-6x11-1

R

F

Kit/Dining
11-8x15-9

Living
11-8x22-0

vaulted clg

Covered Deck
24-0x8-0

plan information

total living area:	1,769
bedrooms:	3
baths:	2
foundation types:	
basement standard	
crawl space	
slab	

special features

- living room boasts an elegant cathedral ceiling and fireplace
- the U-shaped kitchen and dining area combine for easy living
- secondary bedrooms include double closets
- secluded master bedroom features a sloped ceiling, large walk-in closet and private bath

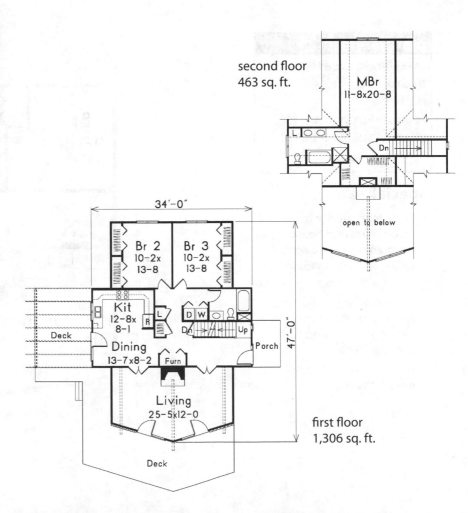

second floor
463 sq. ft.

first floor
1,306 sq. ft.

plan #588-008D-0154

price code AAA

plan information

total living area:	527
bedrooms:	1
baths:	1
foundation type:	
crawl space	

special features

- cleverly arranged home has it all
- foyer spills into the dining nook with access to side views
- an excellent kitchen offers a long breakfast bar and borders the living room with free-standing fireplace
- a cozy bedroom has a full bath just across the hall

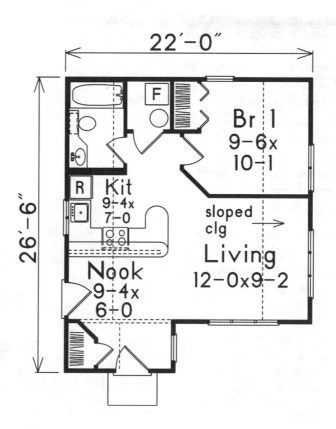

plan #588-016D-0033

price code B

plan information

total living area:	1,563
bedrooms:	3
baths:	2

foundation types:
- basement
- crawl space
- slab

please specify when ordering

special features

- centrally located utility room
- double sliding glass doors add drama to living room
- plenty of storage throughout
- master bedroom is located on the second floor for privacy and includes amenities such as a private rear balcony, dressing area and bath with front balcony

first floor
1,144 sq. ft.

second floor
419 sq. ft.

plan #588-007D-0106

plan information

total living area:	1,200
bedrooms:	2
baths:	1
foundation type:	
walk-out basement	

special features

- entry leads to a large dining area which opens to the kitchen and sun-drenched living room
- an expansive window wall in the two-story atrium lends space and light to living room with fireplace
- the large kitchen features a breakfast bar, built-in pantry and storage galore
- 697 square feet of optional living area on the lower level includes a family room, bedroom #3 and a bath

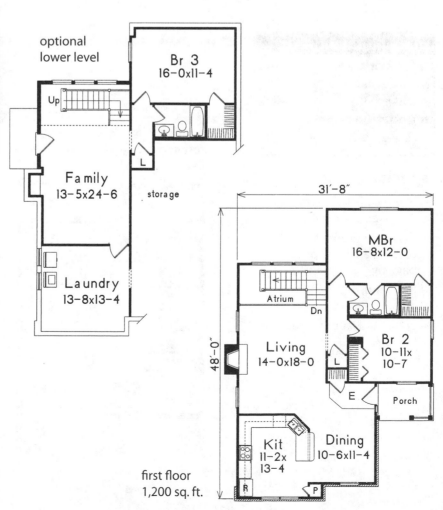

optional lower level

Br 3
16-0x11-4

Up

Family
13-5x24-6

storage

L

Laundry
13-8x13-4

31'-8"

48'-0"

MBr
16-8x12-0

Atrium

Dn

Living
14-0x18-0

L

Br 2
10-11x 10-7

E

Porch

Kit
11-2x 13-4

Dining
10-6x11-4

R

P

first floor
1,200 sq. ft.

order 1-800-367-7667

plan information

total living area:	1,245
bedrooms:	3
baths:	1 1/2
foundation type:	
basement	

special features

- energy efficient home with 2" x 6" exterior walls
- master bedroom has a reading area and private balcony
- bay window brightens living area
- combined laundry area and half bath

second floor
619 sq. ft.

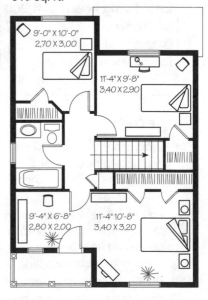

9'-0" X 10'-0"
2,70 X 3,00

11'-4" X 9'-8"
3,40 X 2,90

9'-4" X 6'-8"
2,80 X 2,00

11'-4" 10'-8"
3,40 X 3,20

first floor
626 sq. ft.

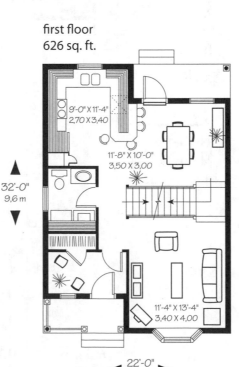

9'-0" X 11'-4"
2,70 X 3,40

11'-8" X 10'-0"
3,50 X 3,00

11'-4" X 13'-4"
3,40 X 4,00

32'-0"
9,6 m

22'-0"
6,6 m

plan #588-038D-0035

plan information

total living area:	1,562
bedrooms:	3
baths:	2
foundation type:	
walk-out basement	

special features

- energy efficient home with 2" x 6" exterior walls
- access the large deck from two sets of French doors which fill the home with sunlight
- kitchen with breakfast bar allows for additional dining space
- unique second floor loft is open to first floor and has a private covered deck
- optional lower level has an additional 678 square feet of living area

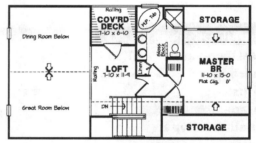

second floor
500 sq. ft.

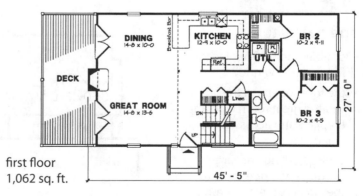

first floor
1,062 sq. ft.

45' - 5"

27' - 0"

optional
lower level

order 1-800-367-7667

plan information

total living area:	1,360
bedrooms:	3
baths:	2
garage:	2-car
foundation type:	
basement	

special features

- double-gabled front facade frames large windows
- the foyer opens to the vaulted great room with a fireplace and access to the rear deck
- vaulted ceiling and large windows add openness to the kitchen/breakfast room
- bedroom #3 easily converts to a den
- plan easily adapts to crawl space or slab construction, with the utilities replacing the stairs

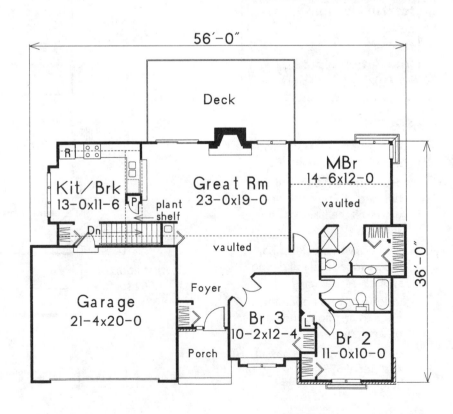

plan #588-055D-0071

plan information

total living area:	1,542
bedrooms:	2
baths:	2

foundation types:
  crawl space
  slab
  please specify when ordering

special features

- den has a vaulted ceiling and walk-around fireplace
- kitchen features an eating bar and island work area
- rear grilling porch with supply room and kitchen access is a convenient feature

second floor
383 sq. ft.

first floor
1,159 sq. ft.

plan information

total living area:	1,609
bedrooms:	3
baths:	2 1/2
garage:	2-car
foundation type:	
slab	

special features

- sunny bay window in breakfast room
- the U-shaped kitchen has a conveniently located pantry
- spacious utility room creates easy access from the garage to the rest of the home
- both bedrooms on the second floor feature dormers
- family room includes plenty of space for entertaining

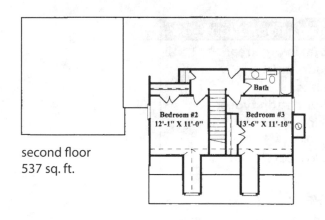

second floor
537 sq. ft.

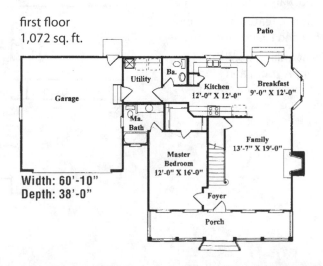

first floor
1,072 sq. ft.

Width: 60'-10"
Depth: 38'-0"

plan #588-058D-0032

plan information

total living area:	1,879
bedrooms:	3
baths:	2
foundation type:	
crawl space	

special features

- open floor plan on both floors makes home appear larger
- loft area overlooks great room or can become an optional fourth bedroom
- large storage in rear of home has access from exterior

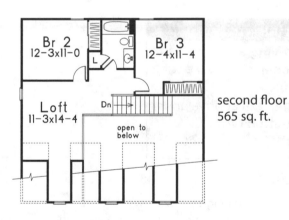

Br 2
12-3x11-0

Br 3
12-4x11-4

Loft
11-3x14-4

Dn

open to below

second floor
565 sq. ft.

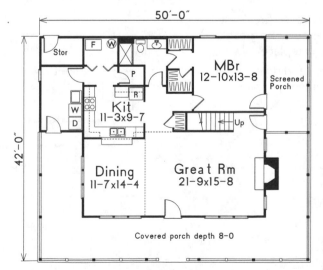

50'-0"

42'-0"

Stor

F W

P

MBr
12-10x13-8

Screened Porch

W
D

Kit
11-3x9-7

R

Up

Dining
11-7x14-4

Great Rm
21-9x15-8

Covered porch depth 8-0

first floor
1,314 sq. ft.

order 1-800-367-7667

plan information

total living area:	1,124
bedrooms:	3
baths:	2
garage:	2-car drive under
foundation type:	
walk-out basement	

special features

- varied ceiling heights throughout this home
- enormous bayed breakfast room overlooks the great room with fireplace
- the washer and dryer closet are conveniently located

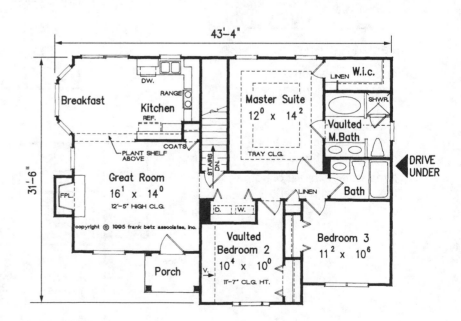

order 1-800-367-7667

plan information

total living area:	1,677
bedrooms:	3
baths:	2
garage:	2-car

foundation types:
  basement
  crawl space
  slab
  please specify when ordering

special features

- energy efficient home with 2" x 6" exterior walls
- master bedroom on first floor for convenience
- skylights enhance second floor bath and covered outdoor deck

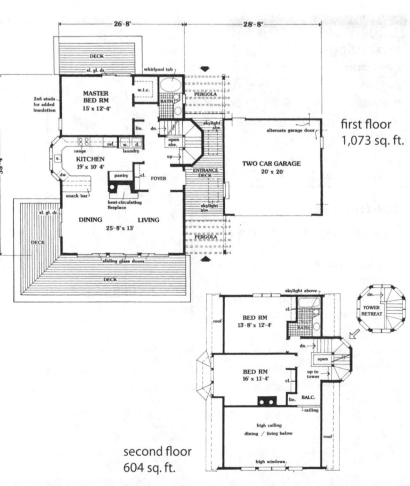

first floor
1,073 sq. ft.

second floor
604 sq. ft.

order 1-800-367-7667

plan information

total living area:	1,642
bedrooms:	3
baths:	2
garage:	2-car
foundation types:	
basement standard	
slab	
crawl space	

special features

- walk-through kitchen boasts a vaulted ceiling and corner sink overlooking the family room
- vaulted family room features a cozy fireplace and access to the rear patio
- master bedroom includes a sloped ceiling, walk-in closet and private bath

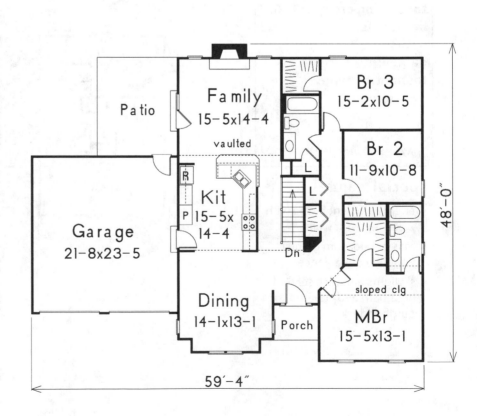

plan #588-007D-0042

plan information

total living area:	914
bedrooms:	2
baths:	1
garage:	2-car drive under
foundation type:	
basement	

special features

- large porch for leisure evenings
- dining area with bay window, open stair and pass-through kitchen create openness
- basement includes generous garage space, storage area, finished laundry and mechanical room

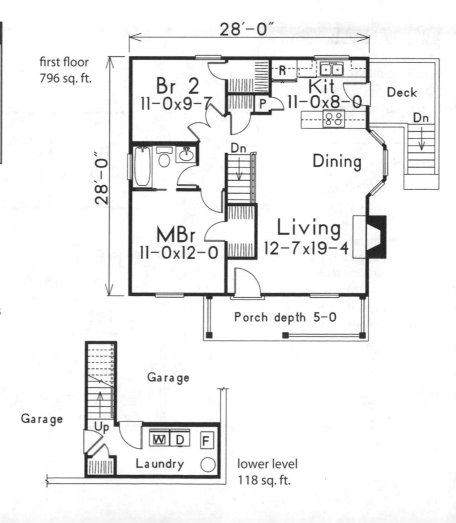

first floor 796 sq. ft.

28'-0"

28'-0"

Br 2
11-0x9-7

Kit
11-0x8-0

R

P

Deck

Dn

Dn

MBr
11-0x12-0

Dining

Living
12-7x19-4

Porch depth 5-0

Garage

Garage

Up

W D F

Laundry

lower level 118 sq. ft.

J.N. HANSEN S.D.G.

plan information

total living area:	962
bedrooms:	2
baths:	1
foundation type:	
crawl space	

special features

- both the kitchen and family room share warmth from the fireplace
- charming facade features a covered porch on one side, screened porch on the other and attractive planter boxes
- the L-shaped kitchen boasts a convenient pantry

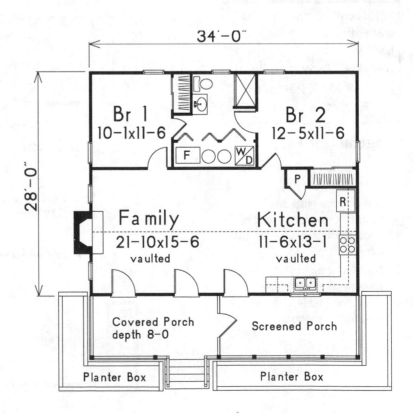

order 1-800-367-7667

plan information

total living area:	800
bedrooms:	2
baths:	1
foundation types:	
crawl space standard basement	

special features

- master bedroom has a walk-in closet and private access to the bath
- large living room features a handy coat closet
- kitchen includes side entrance, closet and convenient laundry area

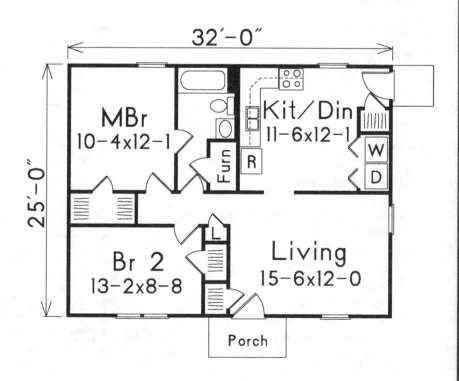

plan #588-078D-0013

price code D

plan information

total living area:	1,175
bedrooms:	2
baths:	2
foundation types:	
basement	
crawl space	
please specify when ordering	

special features

- the two-story living room is brightened by multiple levels of double-hung windows creating a dramatic impression
- the compact kitchen is designed for maximum efficiency
- both bedrooms enjoy privacy and walk-in closets
- the second floor loft area provides a magnificent view of the first floor living space

second floor
375 sq. ft.

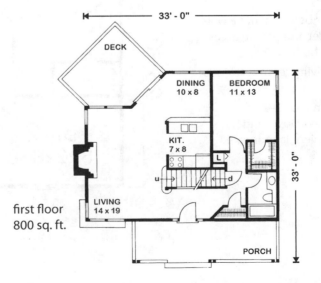

first floor
800 sq. ft.

plan #588-008D-0143

plan information

total living area:	1,299
bedrooms:	3
baths:	2
foundation types:	
crawl space standard	
slab	

special features

- convenient storage for skis, etc. is located outside the front entrance
- the kitchen and dining room receive light from the box-bay window
- large vaulted living room features a cozy fireplace and overlook from the second floor balcony
- second floor balcony extends over the entire length of the living room below

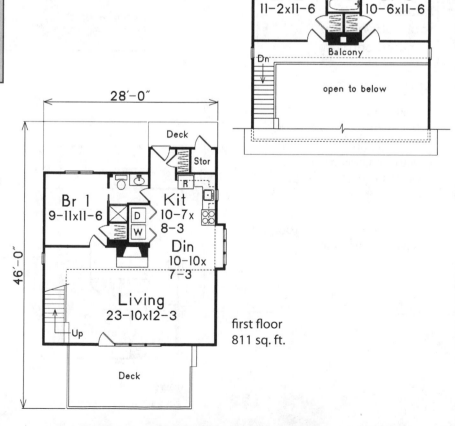

second floor
488 sq. ft.

first floor
811 sq. ft.

plan #588-007D-0039

price code B

plan information

total living area:	1,563
bedrooms:	2
baths:	1 1/2
foundation type:	
basement	

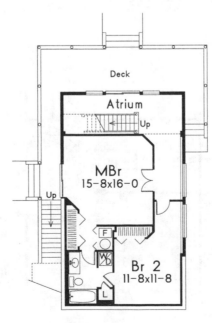

rear view

special features

- enjoyable wrap-around porch and lower sundeck
- vaulted entry is adorned with a palladian window, plant shelves, stone floor and fireplace
- huge vaulted great room has a magnificent view through a two-story atrium window wall

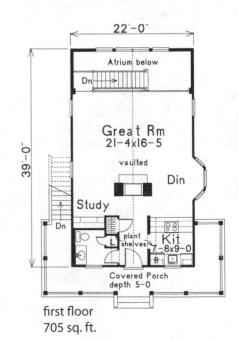

Deck

Atrium

MBr
15-8x16-0

Br 2
11-8x11-8

lower level
858 sq. ft.

22'-0"

Atrium below

Dn

Great Rm
21-4x16-5

vaulted

39'-0"

Study

Din

Dn

plant
shelves

Kit
7-8x9-0

Covered Porch
depth 5-0

first floor
705 sq. ft.

plan #588-008D-0144

price code AA

plan information

total living area:	1,176
bedrooms:	4
baths:	2
foundation types:	
crawl space standard	
slab	

special features

- efficient kitchen offers plenty of storage, a dining area and a stylish eating bar
- a gathering space is created by the large central living room
- closet and storage space throughout helps keep sporting equipment organized and easily accessible
- each end of the home is comprised of two bedrooms and a full bath

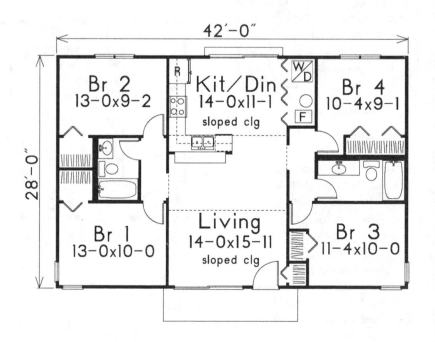

plan #588-021D-0006

price code C

plan information

total living area:	1,600
bedrooms:	3
baths:	2
garage:	2-car side entry
foundation types:	
slab standard	
crawl space	
basement	

special features

- energy efficient home with 2" x 6" exterior walls
- sunken living room features a massive stone fireplace and 16' vaulted ceiling
- the dining room is conveniently located next to the kitchen
- special amenities include a sewing room, glass shelves in the kitchen, a grand master bath and a large utility area
- sunken master bedroom features a sitting room

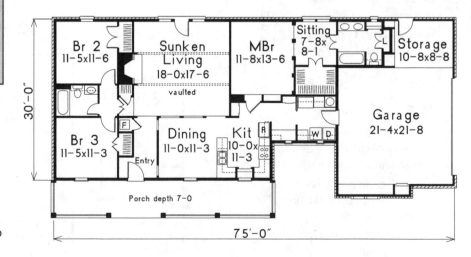

plan #588-007D-0104

plan information

total living area:	969
bedrooms:	2
baths:	1
garage:	1-car rear entry
foundation type:	
walk-out basement	

special features

- eye-pleasing facade enjoys stone accents with country porch for quiet evenings
- a bayed dining area, cozy fireplace and atrium with sunny two-story windows are the many features of the living room
- step-saver kitchen includes a pass-through snack bar
- 325 square feet of optional living area on the lower level

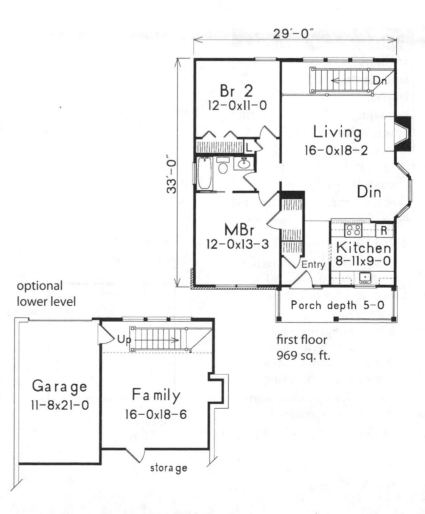

optional lower level

Garage
11-8x21-0

Family
16-0x18-6

storage

29'-0"

33'-0"

Br 2
12-0x11-0

Living
16-0x18-2

Dn

L

MBr
12-0x13-3

Din

Kitchen
8-11x9-0

R

Entry

Porch depth 5-0

first floor
969 sq. ft.

Up

plan #588-038D-0037

price code A

plan information

total living area:	1,434
bedrooms:	3
baths:	2
garage:	2-car
foundation types:	
basement	
crawl space	
slab	
please specify when ordering	

special features

- private second floor master bedroom features a private bath and a roomy walk-in closet
- a country kitchen with peninsula counter adjoins the living room creating the feeling of a larger living area
- the living room has a warm fireplace and a tall ceiling

second floor
416 sq. ft.

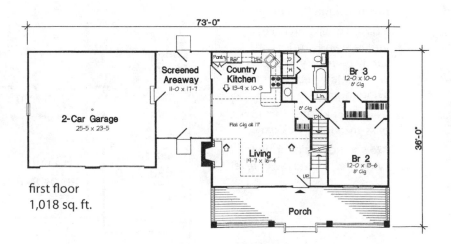

first floor
1,018 sq. ft.

order 1-800-367-7667

plan information

total living area:	720
bedrooms:	2
baths:	1

foundation types:
crawl space standard
slab

special features

- abundant windows in living and dining rooms provide generous sunlight
- secluded laundry area has a handy storage closet
- the U-shaped kitchen with large breakfast bar opens into living area
- large covered deck offers plenty of outdoor living space

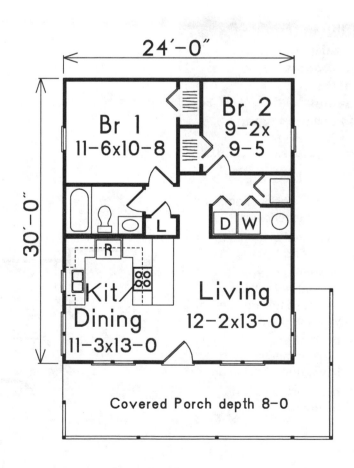

24'-0"

30'-0"

Br 1
11-6x10-8

Br 2
9-2x
9-5

L

R

D W

Kit
Dining
11-3x13-0

Living
12-2x13-0

Covered Porch depth 8-0

plan information

total living area:	1,231
bedrooms:	1
baths:	1
garage:	1-car
foundation type:	
basement	

special features

- energy efficient home with 2" x 6" exterior walls
- nice-sized bedroom is appealing
- enormous bath is highlighted with an oversized tub, double-bowl vanity and separate shower
- family room has a cozy fireplace and spectacular bay window adding drama
- plans include a two bedroom option

2 bedroom option

plan information

total living area:	1,425
bedrooms:	2
baths:	2
foundation types:	
crawl space	
slab	

special features

- great room features a vaulted ceiling and fireplace
- sleeping loft boasts a vaulted ceiling, window seat and bookshelves
- a unique built-in window seat graces the breakfast room
- rear grilling porch includes a cleaning table with built-in sink which is perfect for cleaning game or fish

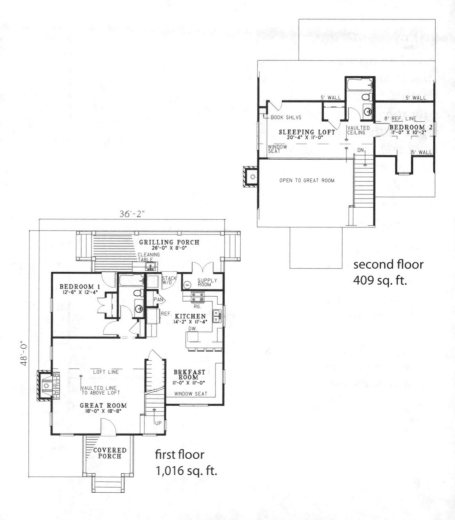

second floor
409 sq. ft.

first floor
1,016 sq. ft.

plan information

total living area:	1,875
bedrooms:	3
baths:	2
garage:	2-car side entry
foundation types:	
crawl space standard	
basement	
slab	

special features

- country-style exterior with wrap-around porch and dormers
- large second floor bedrooms share a dressing area and bath
- master bedroom includes a bay window, walk-in closet, dressing area and bath

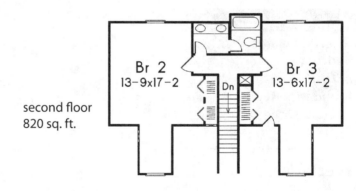

second floor
820 sq. ft.

Br 2
13-9x17-2

Dn

Br 3
13-6x17-2

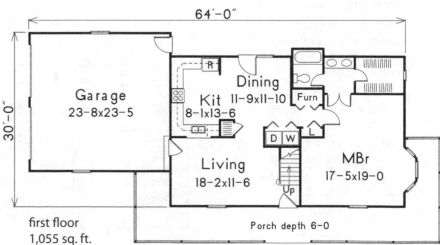

64'-0"

30'-0"

Garage
23-8x23-5

R

Dining
11-9x11-10

Kit
8-1x13-6

Furn

D W L

Living
18-2x11-6

Up

MBr
17-5x19-0

first floor
1,055 sq. ft.

Porch depth 6-0

plan #588-022D-0012

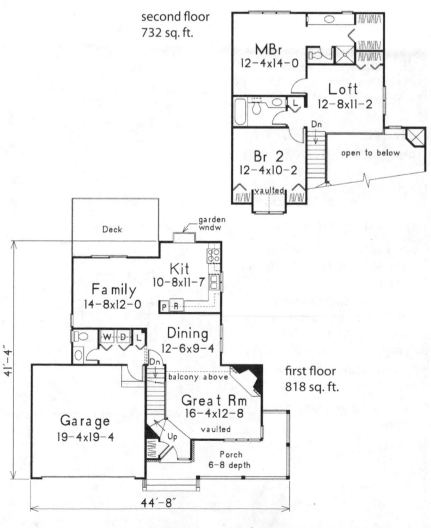

plan information

total living area:	1,550
bedrooms:	2
baths:	2 1/2
garage:	2-car
foundation type:	
basement	

special features

- impressive front entrance with a wrap-around covered porch and raised foyer
- corner fireplace provides a focal point in the vaulted great room
- loft is easily converted to a third bedroom
- large kitchen/family room includes greenhouse windows and access to the deck and utility area
- the secondary bedroom has a large dormer window seat

second floor
732 sq. ft.

MBr
12-4x14-0

Loft
12-8x11-2

Br 2
12-4x10-2

open to below

vaulted

Dn

L

first floor
818 sq. ft.

Deck

garden wndw

Kit
10-8x11-7

Family
14-8x12-0

P R

Dining
12-6x9-4

W D L

Dn

balcony above

Great Rm
16-4x12-8
vaulted

Garage
19-4x19-4

Up

Porch
6-8 depth

41'-4"

44'-8"

plan #588-037D-0006

price code C

plan information

total living area:	1,772
bedrooms:	3
baths:	2
garage:	2-car detached
foundation types:	
slab standard	
crawl space	

special features

- extended porches in front and rear provide a charming touch
- large bay windows lend distinction to the dining room and bedroom #3
- efficient U-shaped kitchen
- master bedroom includes two walk-in closets
- full corner fireplace in family room

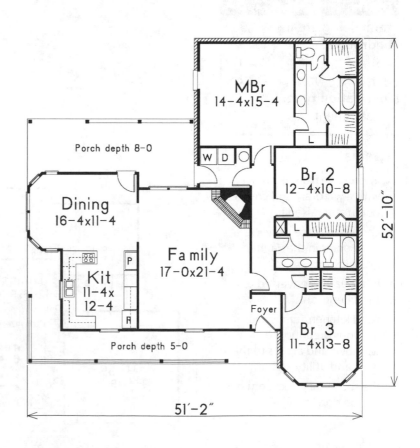

plan #588-016D-0009

plan information

total living area: 1,416
bedrooms: 3
baths: 2
foundation types:
  basement
  crawl space
please specify when ordering

special features

- second floor has a bedroom and bath secluded for privacy
- efficiently designed kitchen accesses deck through sliding glass doors
- wall of windows in dining/living area brightens interior
- enormous wrap-around deck provides plenty of outdoor living area

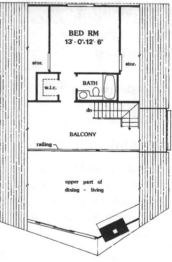

second floor
400 sq. ft.

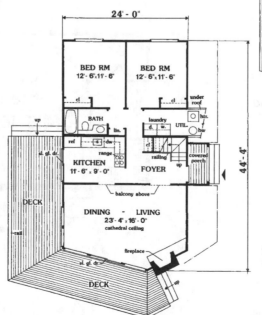

first floor
1,016 sq. ft.

plan #588-007D-0043

price code AAA

plan information

total living area:	647
bedrooms:	1
baths:	1
foundation type:	
crawl space	

special features

- large vaulted room for living/sleeping has plant shelves on each end, stone fireplace and wide glass doors for views
- roomy kitchen is vaulted and has a bayed dining area and fireplace
- step down into a sunken and vaulted bath featuring a 6'-0" whirlpool tub-in-a-bay
- a large palladian window adorns each end of the cottage giving a cheery atmosphere throughout

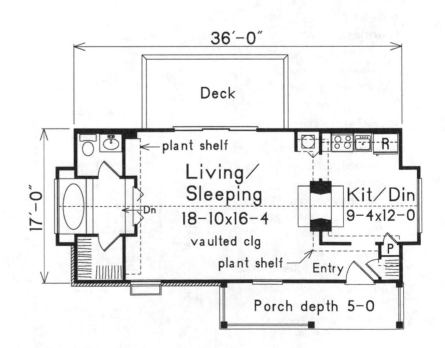

plan #588-001D-0021

price code A

plan information

total living area:	1,416
bedrooms:	3
baths:	2
garage:	2-car
foundation types:	
crawl space standard	
basement	

special features

- excellent floor plan eases traffic
- master bedroom features private bath
- foyer opens to both a formal living room and an informal great room
- great room has access to the outdoors through sliding doors

---

plan #588-008D-0132

price code A

plan information

total living area:	1,209
bedrooms:	3
baths:	2
foundation type:	
crawl space	

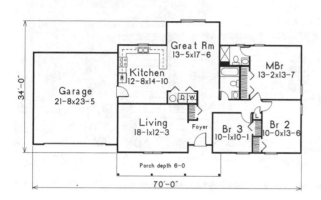

special features

- bracketed shed roof and ski storage add charm to vacation home
- living and dining rooms enjoy a sloped ceiling, second floor balcony overlook and view to a large deck
- kitchen features a snack bar and access to the second floor via a circular staircase
- second floor includes two bedrooms with sizable closets, center hall bath and balcony overlooking rooms below

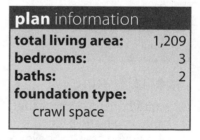

second floor
429 sq. ft.

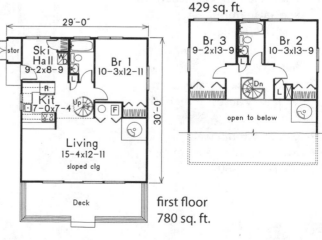

first floor
780 sq. ft.

plan #588-058D-0007

price code AA

plan information

total living area: 1,013
bedrooms: 2
baths: 1
foundation type:
 slab

special features

- vaulted ceilings in both the family room and kitchen with dining area just beyond the breakfast bar

- plant shelf above kitchen is a special feature

- oversized utility room has space for a full-size washer and dryer

- hall bath is centrally located with easy access from both bedrooms

- 2" x 6" exterior walls available, please order plan #588-058D-0073

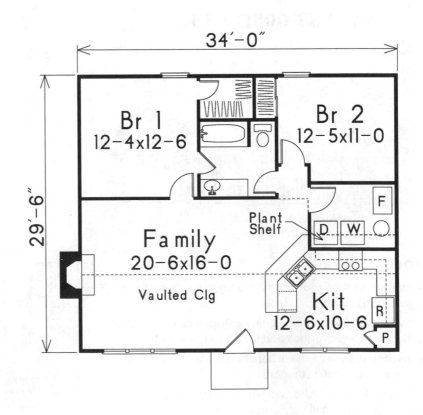

plan #588-016D-0066

price code AA

plan information

total living area:	1,029
bedrooms:	1
baths:	1
garage:	3-car drive under
foundation type:	
slab	

first floor
1,029 sq. ft.

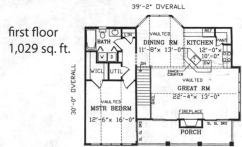

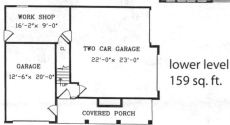

lower level
159 sq. ft.

special features

- luxurious amenities are provided throughout the home including a walk-in closet, large pantry and spacious work shop
- vaulted ceilings throughout add spaciousness
- bath includes utility closet for convenience
- snack counter in kitchen overlooks into vaulted great room

---

plan #588-052D-0011

price code A

plan information

total living area:	1,325
bedrooms:	3
baths:	2
garage:	2-car drive under
foundation types:	
basement	
crawl space	
please specify when ordering	

special features

- sloped ceiling and a fireplace in the living area create a cozy feeling
- formal dining and breakfast areas have an efficiently designed kitchen between them
- master bedroom has a walk-in closet and luxurious private bath

plan information

total living area:	2,030
bedrooms:	3
baths:	2 1/2
foundation types:	
basement	
crawl space	
please specify when ordering	

special features

- energy efficient home with 2" x 6" exterior walls
- centrally located kitchen serves the formal dining room and bayed breakfast room with ease
- spacious living room is warmed by a grand fireplace
- the second floor bedrooms are generously sized and each feature built-in desk areas

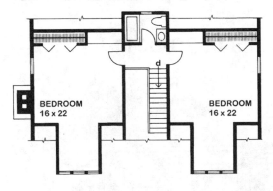

BEDROOM
16 x 22

BEDROOM
16 x 22

second floor
735 sq. ft.

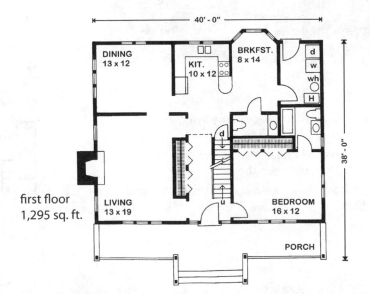

40' - 0"

DINING
13 x 12

KIT.
10 x 12

BRKFST.
8 x 14

38' - 0"

LIVING
13 x 19

BEDROOM
16 x 12

first floor
1,295 sq. ft.

PORCH

plan #588-017D-0008

price code B

plan information

total living area:	1,466
bedrooms:	3
baths:	2
garage:	2-car
foundation types:	
basement standard	
slab	

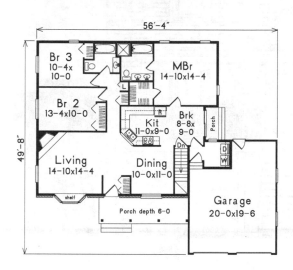

56'-4"

49'-8"

Br 3
10-4x
10-0

MBr
14-10x14-4

Br 2
13-4x10-0

Kit
11-0x9-0

Brk
8-8x
9-0

Porch

Living
14-10x14-4

Dining
10-0x11-0

Dn

D
W

shelf

Porch depth 6-0

Garage
20-0x19-6

special features

- energy efficient home with 2" x 6" exterior walls
- foyer separates the living room from the dining room and contains a generous coat closet
- large living room features a corner fireplace, bay window and pass-through to the kitchen
- informal breakfast area opens to a large terrace through sliding glass doors which brighten the area
- master bedroom has a large walk-in closet and private bath

---

plan #588-001D-0035

price code A

plan information

total living area:	1,396
bedrooms:	3
baths:	2
garage:	1-car rear entry
	carport
foundation types:	
basement standard	
crawl space	

special features

- gabled front adds interest to the facade
- living and dining rooms share a vaulted ceiling
- master bedroom features a walk-in closet and private bath
- functional kitchen boasts a center work island and convenient pantry

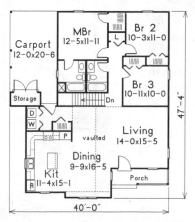

Carport
12-0x20-6

MBr
12-5x11-11

Br 2
10-3x11-0

Storage

Br 3
10-11x10-0

Dn

D
W
P

vaulted

Living
14-0x15-5

Kit
11-4x15-1

Dining
9-9x16-5

Porch

47'-4"

40'-0"

plan #588-024D-0008

price code B

plan information

total living area:	1,650
bedrooms:	4
baths:	2
foundation type:	
pier	

special features

- master bedroom is located on the second floor for privacy
- open living area connects to the dining area
- two-story living area features lots of windows for views to the outdoors and a large fireplace
- efficiently designed kitchen

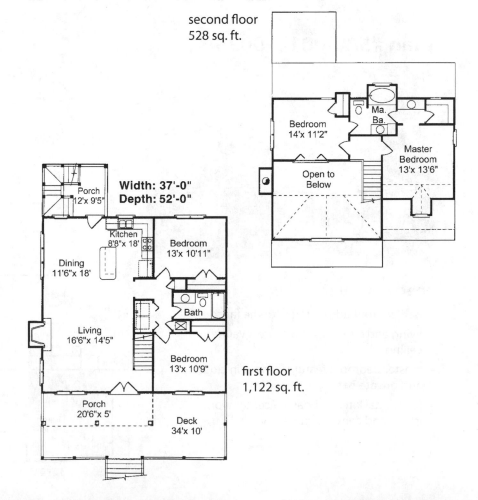

second floor
528 sq. ft.

first floor
1,122 sq. ft.

Width: 37'-0"
Depth: 52'-0"

plan #588-022D-0019

price code A

plan information

total living area:	1,283
bedrooms:	3
baths:	2
garage:	2-car
foundation type:	
basement	

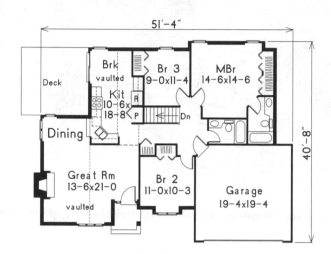

special features

- vaulted breakfast room has sliding doors that open onto deck
- kitchen features convenient corner sink and pass-through to dining room
- open living atmosphere in dining area and great room
- vaulted great room features a fireplace

---

plan #588-045D-0015

price code A

plan information

total living area:	977
bedrooms:	2
baths:	1 1/2
garage:	1-car
foundation type:	
basement	

special features

- comfortable living room features a vaulted ceiling, fireplace, plant shelf and coat closet
- both bedrooms are located on the second floor and share a bath with double-bowl vanity and linen closet
- sliding glass doors in the dining room provide access to the deck

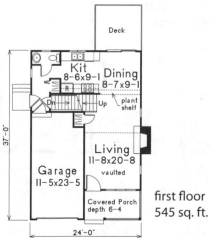

second floor
432 sq. ft.

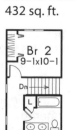

first floor
545 sq. ft.

plan #588-021D-0016

price code B

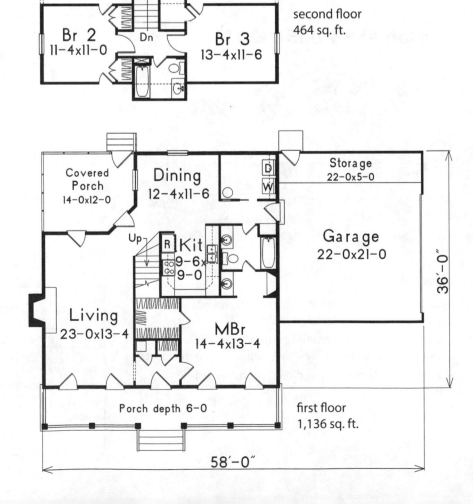

second floor
464 sq. ft.

plan information

total living area:	1,600
bedrooms:	3
baths:	2
garage:	2-car side entry
foundation types:	

    crawl space standard
    slab

special features

- energy efficient home with 2" x 6" exterior walls

- first floor master bedroom is accessible from two points of entry

- master bath dressing area includes separate vanities and a mirrored makeup counter

- second floor bedrooms have generous storage space and share a full bath

Attic

Br 2
11-4x11-0

Dn

Attic

Br 3
13-4x11-6

Covered Porch
14-0x12-0

Dining
12-4x11-6

Storage
22-0x5-0

Up

Kit
9-6x
9-0

Garage
22-0x21-0

Living
23-0x13-4

MBr
14-4x13-4

36'-0"

Porch depth 6-0

first floor
1,136 sq. ft.

58'-0"

plan #588-001D-0018

price code AA

plan information

total living area:	988
bedrooms:	3
baths:	1
garage:	1-car
foundation types:	
basement standard	
crawl space	

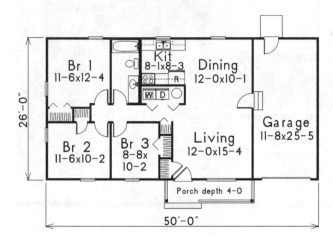

special features

- pleasant covered porch entry
- the kitchen, living and dining areas are combined to maximize space
- the entry has a convenient coat closet
- laundry closet is located adjacent to bedrooms

---

plan #588-007D-0029

price code AAA

plan information

total living area:	576
bedrooms:	1
baths:	1
foundation type:	
crawl space	

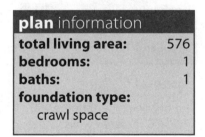

special features

- perfect country retreat features vaulted living room and entry with skylights and a plant shelf above
- a double-door entry leads to the vaulted bedroom with bath access
- kitchen offers generous storage and pass-through breakfast bar

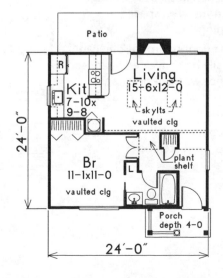

plan information

total living area:	1,487
bedrooms:	3
baths:	1 1/2
foundation type:	
basement	

special features

- energy efficient home with 2" x 6" exterior walls
- kitchen has a pass-through counter with space for dining
- first floor bedroom/den can easily be converted to an office with spacious walk-in closet and access to deck outdoors
- second floor bedroom also has a private deck

second floor
576 sq. ft.

first floor
911 sq. ft.

plan #588-008D-0072

price code A

plan information

total living area:	1,200
bedrooms:	2
baths:	2
foundation type:	
crawl space	

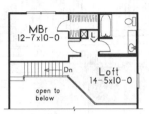

second floor
416 sq. ft.

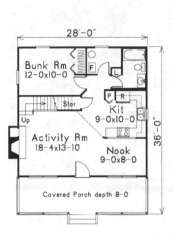

first floor
784 sq. ft.

special features

- enjoy lazy summer evenings on this magnificent porch
- activity area has a fireplace and ascending stair from the cozy loft
- kitchen features a built-in pantry
- master bedroom enjoys a large bath, walk-in closet and cozy loft overlooking the room below

---

plan #588-032D-0005

price code AA

plan information

total living area:	994
bedrooms:	2
baths:	1
foundation type:	
basement	

special features

- energy efficient home with 2" x 6" exterior walls
- beautiful and sunny dining area
- kitchen has center island ideal for food preparation as well as additional dining
- plenty of closets and storage throughout

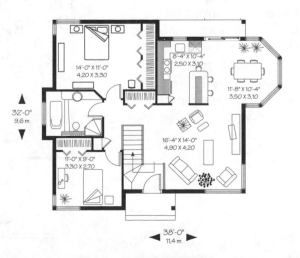

order 1-800-367-7667

plan information

total living area:	1,230
bedrooms:	3
baths:	1
foundation types:	
crawl space standard	
slab	

special features

- spacious living room accesses huge deck
- bedroom #3 features a balcony overlooking the deck
- kitchen with dining area accesses the outdoors
- washer and dryer are tucked under the stairs for space efficiency

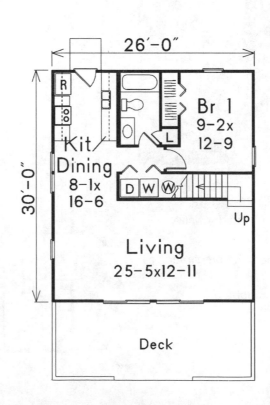

26'-0"

30'-0"

R

Kit
Dining
8-1x
16-6

Br 1
9-2x
12-9

L

D W W

Living
25-5x12-11

Up

Deck

first floor
780 sq. ft.

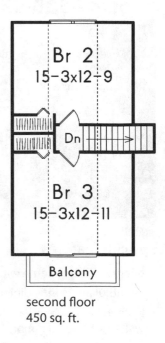

Br 2
15-3x12-9

Dn

Br 3
15-3x12-11

Balcony

second floor
450 sq. ft.

plan #588-045D-0010

price code B

plan information

total living area:	1,558
bedrooms:	2
baths:	2
garage:	2-car rear entry
foundation type:	
basement	

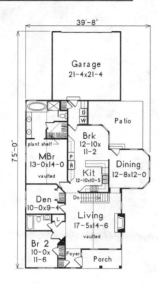

special features

- illuminated spaces are created by visual access to the outdoor living areas
- vaulted master bedroom features a private bath with whirlpool tub, separate shower and large walk-in closet
- convenient laundry area has garage access
- practical den or third bedroom is perfect for a variety of uses
- the U-shaped kitchen is adjacent to the sunny breakfast area

---

plan #588-049D-0005

price code A

plan information

total living area:	1,389
bedrooms:	3
baths:	2
garage:	2-car
foundation type:	
slab	

special features

- energy efficient home with 2" x 6" exterior walls
- formal living room has a warming fireplace and delightful bay window
- the U-shaped kitchen shares a snack bar with the bayed family room
- lovely master bedroom has its own private bath

order 1-800-367-7667

plan information

total living area:	1,124
bedrooms:	2
baths:	1
garage:	1-car
foundation type:	
basement	

special features

- energy efficient home with 2" x 6" exterior walls
- wrap-around porch creates an outdoor living area
- large dining area easily accommodates extra guests
- sunken family room becomes a cozy retreat

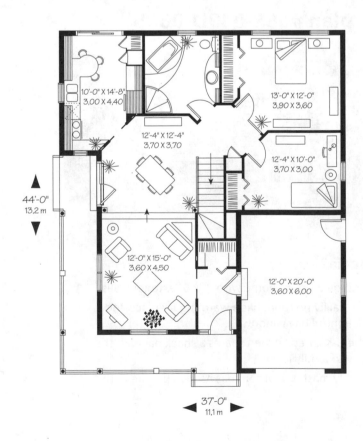

plan #588-013D-0001

price code AA

plan information

total living area:	1,050
bedrooms:	3
baths:	2
garage:	1-car
foundation types:	
basement	
slab	
please specify when ordering	

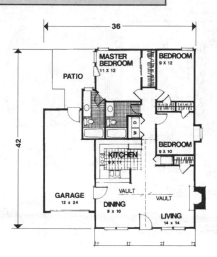

special features

- master bedroom has its own private bath and access to the outdoors onto a private patio
- vaulted ceilings in the living and dining areas create a feeling of spaciousness
- the laundry closet is convenient to all bedrooms
- efficient U-shaped kitchen

---

plan #588-014D-0005

price code A

plan information

total living area:	1,314
bedrooms:	3
baths:	2
garage:	2-car
foundation type:	
basement	

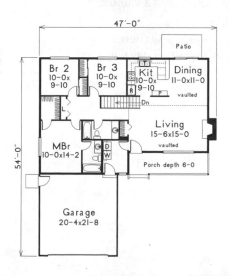

special features

- energy efficient home with 2" x 6" exterior walls
- covered porch adds immediate appeal and welcoming charm
- open floor plan combined with a vaulted ceiling offers spacious living
- functional kitchen is complete with a pantry and eating bar
- cozy fireplace in the living room
- private master bedroom features a large walk-in closet and bath

plan information

total living area:	717
bedrooms:	1
baths:	1
foundation type:	
slab	

special features

- incline ladder leads up to cozy loft area
- living room features plenty of windows and a vaulted ceiling
- the U-shaped kitchen includes a small bay window at the sink

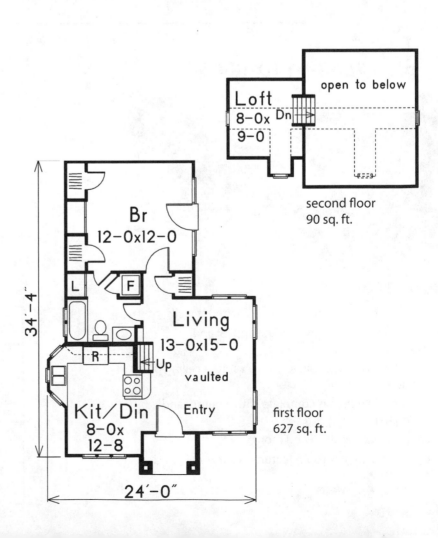

second floor
90 sq. ft.

first floor
627 sq. ft.

plan #588-017D-0005

price code B

plan information

total living area:	1,367
bedrooms:	3
baths:	2
garage:	2-car
foundation types:	
basement standard	
slab	

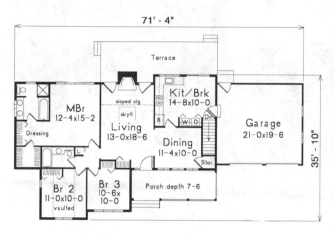

71' - 4"

35' - 10"

Terrace

MBr 12-4x15-2

sloped clg

skylt

Living 13-0x18-6

Kit/Brk 14-8x10-0

Dining 11-4x10-0

Garage 21-0x19-6

Stor.

Dressing

Br 2 11-0x10-0 vaulted

Br 3 10-6x 10-0

Porch depth 7-6

special features

- energy efficient home with 2" x 6" exterior walls
- neat front porch shelters the entrance
- dining room has a full wall of windows and convenient storage area
- breakfast area leads to the rear terrace through sliding doors
- the large living room features a high ceiling, skylight and fireplace

---

plan #588-028D-0009

price code C

plan information

total living area:	2,189
bedrooms:	3
baths:	2 1/2
garage:	2-car detached
foundation types:	
crawl space	
slab	
please specify when ordering	

special features

- study could easily be converted to a fourth bedroom
- secluded master bedroom has all the luxuries for comfortable living
- all bedrooms include spacious walk-in closets

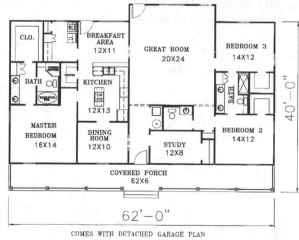

CLO.

BREAKFAST AREA 12X11

GREAT ROOM 20X24

BEDROOM 3 14X12

BATH

KITCHEN 12X13

BATH

MASTER BEDROOM 16X14

DINING ROOM 12X10

STUDY 12X8

BEDROOM 2 14X12

COVERED PORCH 62X6

40'—0"

62'—0"

COMES WITH DETACHED GARAGE PLAN

plan #588-053D-0041

price code A

plan information

total living area:	1,364
bedrooms:	3
baths:	2
garage:	2-car drive under
foundation type:	
basement	

special features

- master bedroom includes a full bath
- pass-through kitchen opens into breakfast room with laundry closet and access to deck
- adjoining dining and living rooms with vaulted ceilings and a fireplace create an open living area
- dining room features a large bay window

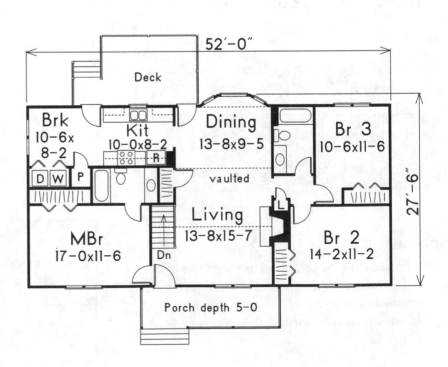

plan #588-008D-0133

price code AAA

plan information

total living area:	624
bedrooms:	2
baths:	1
foundation type:	
pier	

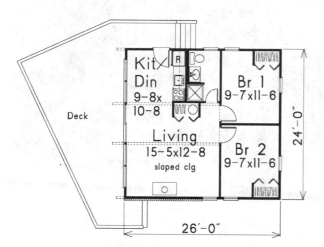

special features

- the combination of stone, vertical siding, lots of glass and a low roof line creates a cozy retreat
- vaulted living area features a free-standing fireplace that heats the adjacent stone wall
- efficient kitchen includes a dining area and view onto an angular deck
- two bedrooms share a hall bath with shower

---

plan #588-007D-0045

price code A

special features

- rear entry garage and elongated brick wall add to the appealing facade
- dramatic vaulted living room includes corner fireplace and towering feature windows
- breakfast room is immersed in light from two large windows and glass sliding doors

plan information

total living area:	1,321
bedrooms:	3
baths:	2
garage:	1-car rear entry
foundation type:	
basement	

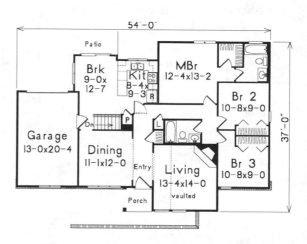

83

plan #588-058D-0013

order 1-800-367-7667

plan information

total living area:	1,073
bedrooms:	2
baths:	1
foundation type:	
crawl space	

special features

- home includes a lovely covered front porch and a screened porch off the dining area
- attractive box window brightens the kitchen
- space for an efficiency washer and dryer is located conveniently between the bedrooms
- family room is spotlighted by a fireplace with flanking bookshelves and spacious vaulted ceiling

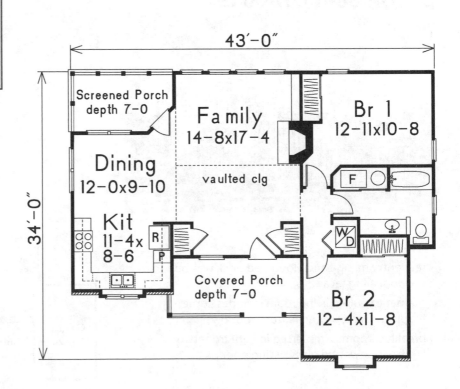

43'-0"

34'-0"

Screened Porch
depth 7-0

Family
14-8x17-4

Br 1
12-11x10-8

Dining
12-0x9-10

vaulted clg

Kit
11-4x
8-6

F

W
D

Covered Porch
depth 7-0

Br 2
12-4x11-8

plan #588-016D-0041

plan information

total living area: 1,097
bedrooms: 3
baths: 2
garage: optional 2-car side entry
foundation types:
  basement
  crawl space
  slab
  please specify when ordering

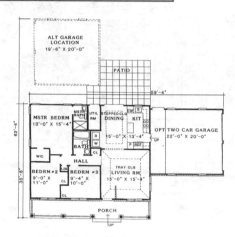

special features

- the U-shaped kitchen wraps around center island
- master bedroom includes its own private bath and walk-in closet
- living room provides expansive view to the rear

---

plan #588-047D-0003

price code A

plan information

total living area: 1,442
bedrooms: 3
baths: 2
garage: 2-car side entry carport
foundation type:
  slab

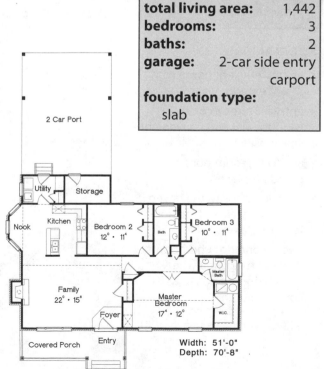

special features

- utility room includes extra counterspace and a closet for storage
- kitchen has a useful center island creating extra workspace
- vaulted master bedroom has unique double-door entry, private bath and a walk-in closet

plan information

total living area:	1,635
bedrooms:	3
baths:	2
foundation type:	
crawl space	

special features

- energy efficient home with 2" x 6" exterior walls
- entry features a cozy window seat and convenient coat closet
- airy living room boasts a grand fireplace
- kitchen opens to the bayed breakfast area and includes a laundry closet
- two second floor bedrooms flank a sitting area where French doors open to a covered porch

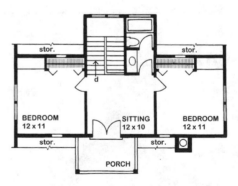

second floor
555 sq. ft.

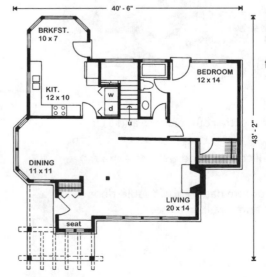

first floor
1,080 sq. ft.

plan #588-017D-0009

price code B

plan information

total living area:	1,432
bedrooms:	3
baths:	2
garage:	1-car
foundation types:	
basement standard	
slab	

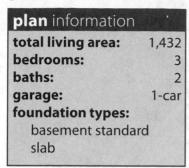

second floor
465 sq. ft.

first floor
967 sq. ft.

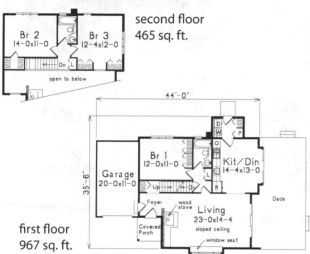

special features

- energy efficient home with 2" x 6" exterior walls
- enter the two-story foyer from the covered porch or garage
- living room has a square bay window with seat, glazed end wall with floor-to-ceiling windows and access to the deck
- kitchen/dining room also opens to the deck for added convenience

---

plan #588-001D-0081

price code AA

special features

- the U-shaped kitchen includes a breakfast bar and convenient laundry area
- master bedroom features private half bath and large closet
- dining room has outdoor access
- dining and great rooms combine to create an open living atmosphere

plan information

total living area:	1,160
bedrooms:	3
baths:	1 1/2
foundation types:	
crawl space standard	
basement	
slab	

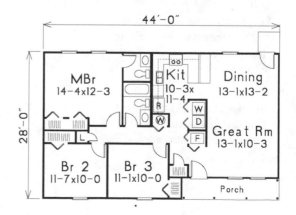

87

plan information

total living area:	1,560
bedrooms:	3
baths:	2
garage:	2-car
foundation type:	
slab	

special features

- cozy breakfast room is tucked at the rear of this home and features plenty of windows for natural light
- large entry has easy access to the secondary bedrooms, utility area, and dining and living rooms
- private master bedroom
- kitchen overlooks the living room which features a fireplace and patio access

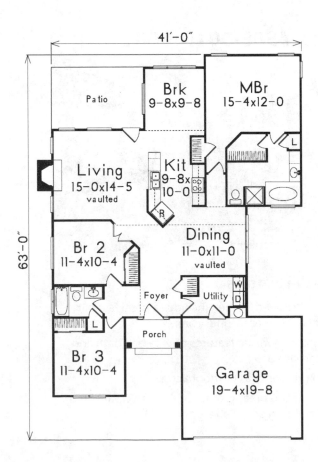

plan #588-032D-0007

price code AA

plan information

total living area:	1,053
bedrooms:	3
baths:	1
foundation type:	
basement	

special features

- energy efficient home with 2" x 6" exterior walls
- spacious kitchen and dining room
- roomy bath includes an oversized tub
- entry has a handy coat closet

---

plan #588-055D-0019

price code AA

plan information

total living area:	985
bedrooms:	2
baths:	1
garage:	2-car rear entry
foundation types:	
crawl space	
slab	
please specify when ordering	

special features

- breakfast room combines with kitchen for a cozy eating space
- the large laundry area is tucked at the back of this home near the kitchen for convenience
- charming covered front entry

plan #588-022D-0002

plan information

total living area:	1,246
bedrooms:	3
baths:	2
garage:	2-car
foundation type:	
basement	

special features

- corner living room window adds openness and light
- out-of-the-way kitchen with dining area accesses the outdoors
- private first floor master bedroom has a corner window
- large walk-in closet is located in bedroom #3
- easily built perimeter allows economical construction

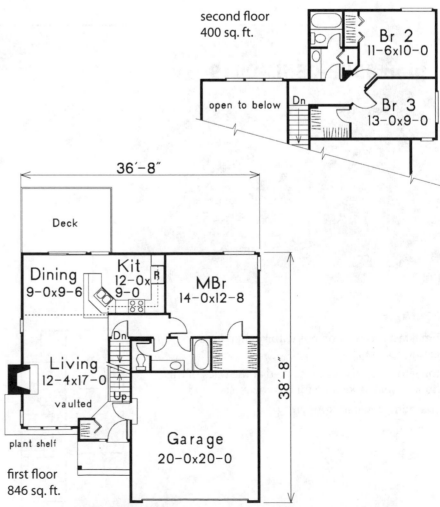

second floor
400 sq. ft.

Br 2
11-6x10-0

open to below

Dn

Br 3
13-0x9-0

36'-8"

Deck

Dining
9-0x9-6

Kit
12-0x
9-0

MBr
14-0x12-8

38'-8"

Living
12-4x17-0

vaulted

Dn

Up

Garage
20-0x20-0

plant shelf

first floor
846 sq. ft.

plan #588-008D-0158

price code B

plan information

total living area:	1,584
bedrooms:	3
baths:	2
foundation types:	

partial basement/crawl
space standard
crawl space

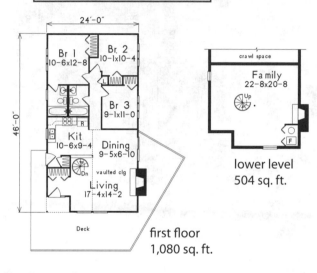

24'-0"

46'-0"

Br 1
10-6x12-8

Br. 2
10-1x10-4

Br 3
9-1x11-0

Kit
10-6x9-4

Dining
9-5x6-10

vaulted clg

Living
17-4x14-2

Dn

Deck

**first floor
1,080 sq. ft.**

crawl space

Family
22-8x20-8

Up

**lower level
504 sq. ft.**

special features

- vaulted living and dining rooms feature a stone fireplace, ascending spiral staircase and a separate vestibule with guest closet
- space-saving kitchen has an eat-in area and access to the deck
- bedroom #1 has private access to a full bath

---

plan #588-024D-0002

price code A

special features

- compact design has all the luxuries of a larger home
- master bedroom has its privacy away from other bedrooms
- living room has corner fireplace, access to the outdoors and easily reaches the dining area and kitchen
- large utility room has access to the outdoors

plan information

total living area:	1,405
bedrooms:	3
baths:	2
foundation type:	

slab

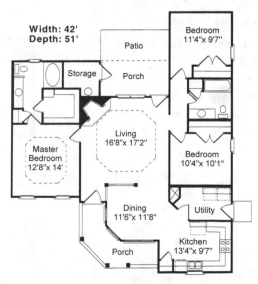

**Width: 42'
Depth: 51'**

Patio

Storage

Porch

Bedroom
11'4"x 9'7"

Living
16'8"x 17'2"

Master
Bedroom
12'8"x 14'

Bedroom
10'4"x 10'1"

Dining
11'6"x 11'8"

Utility

Porch

Kitchen
13'4"x 9'7"

plan #588-039D-0011

price code B

plan information

total living area:	1,780
bedrooms:	3
baths:	2 1/2
garage:	2-car
foundation types:	
basement	
crawl space	
slab	
please specify when ordering	

special features

- traditional styling with all the comforts of home
- first floor master bedroom has a walk-in closet and bath
- large kitchen and dining area opens to the deck

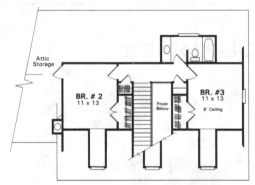

second floor
551 sq. ft.

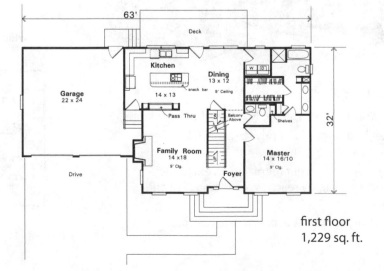

first floor
1,229 sq. ft.

plan #588-028D-0001

price code AAA

plan information

total living area:	864
bedrooms:	2
baths:	1
foundation types:	
crawl space	
slab	
please specify when ordering	

special features

- large laundry area accesses the outdoors as well as the kitchen
- front covered porch creates an ideal outdoor living area
- snack bar in kitchen creates a quick and easy dining area

---

plan #588-037D-0002

price code C

plan information

total living area:	1,816
bedrooms:	3
baths:	2 1/2
garage:	2-car detached
foundation types:	
slab standard	
crawl space	

special features

- the living room features a two-way fireplace with nearby window seat
- wrap-around dining room windows create a sunroom appearance
- master bedroom has an abundant closet and storage space
- rear dormers, closets and desk areas create an interesting and functional second floor

second floor
486 sq. ft.

first floor
1,330 sq. ft.

order 1-800-367-7667

plan information

total living area:	1,577
bedrooms:	3
baths:	2 1/2
foundation type:	
crawl space	

special features

- large living area is a great gathering place with an enormous stone fireplace, cathedral ceiling and kitchen with snack bar nearby
- second floor loft has a half-wall creating an open atmosphere
- the large utility room creates workspace

← 48' - 0" →

Redwood Deck

DN   DN

MstrBed
13x14

Living Area
22x14
Cathedral Clg.

first floor
1,301 sq. ft.

Bed#2
13x9

28' - 0"

UP   UP 7"

Snack Bar

UP 7"

Ent   **Kit**
12x9

Util

Bed#3
13x11

Redwood Deck

DN

Open To Living Area Below.

DN   Half Wall

Loft
13x12
7'-6" Clg.

second floor
276 sq. ft.

Redwood Deck

plan #588-015D-0023

price code B

plan information

total living area:	1,649
bedrooms:	4
baths:	2 1/2
garage:	2-car side entry
foundation types:	
basement	
crawl space	

please specify when ordering

Width: 30'-0"
Depth: 52'-0"

first floor
858 sq. ft.

second floor
791 sq. ft.

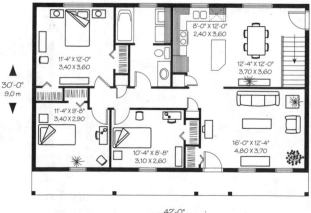

special features

- energy efficient home with 2" x 6" exterior walls
- ideal design for a narrow lot
- country kitchen includes an island and eating bar
- master bedroom has a 12' vaulted ceiling and a charming arched window

---

plan #588-032D-0001

price code AA

plan information

total living area:	1,092
bedrooms:	3
baths:	1
foundation type:	
basement	

special features

- energy efficient home with 2"x 6" exterior walls
- sunken family room adds interest
- nice-sized bedrooms are convenient to the bath
- handy work island in kitchen

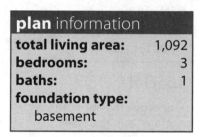

30'-0"
9,0 m

42'-0"
12,6 m

plan information

total living area:	1,700
bedrooms:	3
baths:	1 1/2
foundation type:	
basement	

special features

- energy efficient home with 2" x 6" exterior walls
- cozy living area has plenty of space for entertaining
- snack bar in kitchen provides extra dining area

second floor
840 sq. ft.

11'-8" X 11'-0"
3,50 X 3,30

13'-0" X 14'-0"
3,90 X 4,20

11'-0" X 11'-0"
3,30 X 3,30

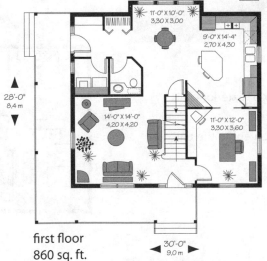

11'-0" X 10'-0"
3,30 X 3,00

9'-0" X 14'-4"
2,70 X 4,30

28'-0"
8,4 m

14'-0" X 14'-0"
4,20 X 4,20

11'-0" X 12'-0"
3,30 X 3,60

first floor
860 sq. ft.

30'-0"
9,0 m

plan #588-035D-0008

price code A

plan information

total living area:	1,215
bedrooms:	3
baths:	2
garage:	2-car

foundation types:
walk-out basement
crawl space
slab
please specify when ordering

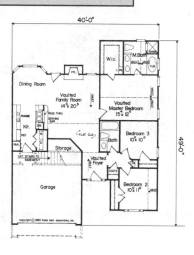

special features

- serving bar counter extends kitchen into living area
- convenient front hall bath
- vaulted master bedroom has a spacious walk-in closet and private bath
- efficient galley-styled kitchen has everything within reach

---

plan #588-039D-0002

price code A

plan information

total living area:	1,333
bedrooms:	3
baths:	2
garage:	2-car carport

foundation types:
crawl space
slab
please specify when ordering

special features

- country charm with a covered front porch
- dining area looks into the family room with fireplace
- master suite has a walk-in closet and private bath

Width: 55'-6"
Depth: 64'-3"

plan information

total living area:	581
bedrooms:	1
baths:	1
foundation type:	
slab	

special features

- kitchen/living room features space for dining and spiral steps leading to the loft area
- large loft area can easily be converted to a bedroom or home office
- entry space has a unique built-in display niche

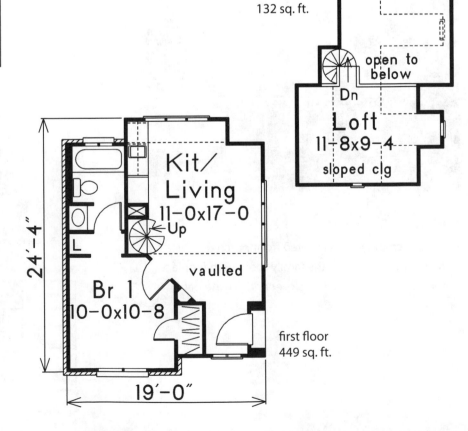

second floor
132 sq. ft.

open to below

Dn

Loft
11-8x9-4

sloped clg

Kit/
Living
11-0x17-0
Up

vaulted

Br 1
10-0x10-8

24'-4"

19'-0"

first floor
449 sq. ft.

plan #588-024D-0005

price code B

plan information

total living area:	1,649
bedrooms:	3
baths:	2
foundation type:	
pier	

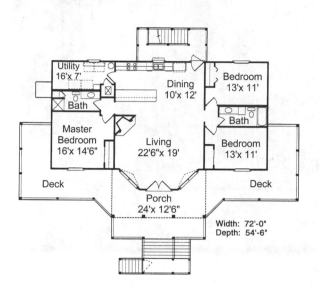

Width: 72'-0"
Depth: 54'-6"

special features

- enormous two-story living room has lots of windows and double-door access onto a spacious porch
- master bedroom is separated from other bedrooms for privacy
- well-organized kitchen has an abundance of counterspace for serving and dining

---

plan #588-052D-0048

price code C

plan information

total living area:	1,870
bedrooms:	3
baths:	2 1/2
garage:	2-car drive under
foundation type:	
basement	

special features

- kitchen is open to the living and dining areas
- breakfast area has a cathedral ceiling creating a sunroom effect
- master bedroom is spacious with all the amenities
- second floor bedrooms share hall bath

second floor
711 sq. ft.

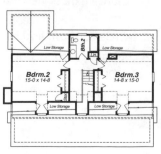

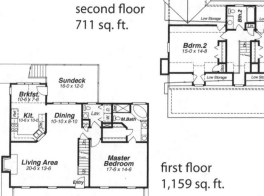

first floor
1,159 sq. ft.

plan #588-022D-0001

price code AA

plan information

total living area:	1,039
bedrooms:	2
baths:	1 1/2
foundation type:	
crawl space	

special features

- cathedral construction provides the maximum in living area openness
- expansive glass viewing walls
- two decks, front and back
- charming second story loft arrangement
- simple, low-maintenance construction

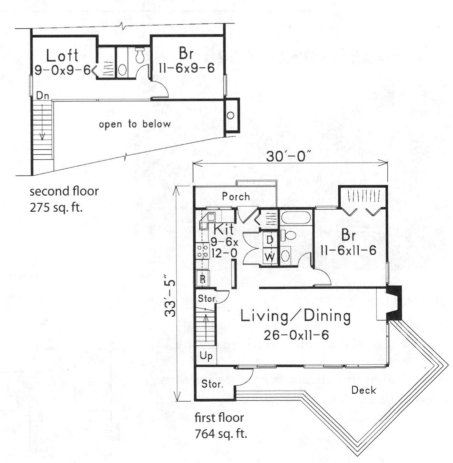

second floor
275 sq. ft.

first floor
764 sq. ft.

plan #588-008D-0136

price code AA

plan information

total living area:	1,106
bedrooms:	2
baths:	1
foundation type:	
pier	

first floor
792 sq. ft.

second floor
314 sq. ft.

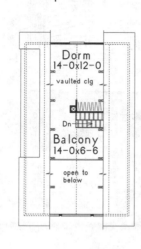

special features

- delightful A-frame provides exciting vacation-style living all year long
- deck accesses a large living room with an open soaring ceiling
- enormous sleeping area is provided on the second floor with balcony overlook to living room below

---

plan #588-038D-0018

price code B

special features

- energy efficient home with 2" x 6" exterior walls
- master bedroom has a private bath and large walk-in closet
- a central stone fireplace and windows on two walls are focal points in the living room
- decorative beams and sloped ceilings add interest to the kitchen, living and dining rooms

plan information

total living area:	1,792
bedrooms:	3
baths:	2
garage:	2-car drive under
foundation type:	
basement	

plan information

total living area:	1,399
bedrooms:	3
baths:	1 1/2
garage:	1-car
foundation types:	
basement standard	
crawl space	
slab	

special features

- living room overlooks the dining area through arched columns

- laundry room contains a handy half bath

- spacious master bedroom includes a sitting area, walk-in closet and plenty of sunlight

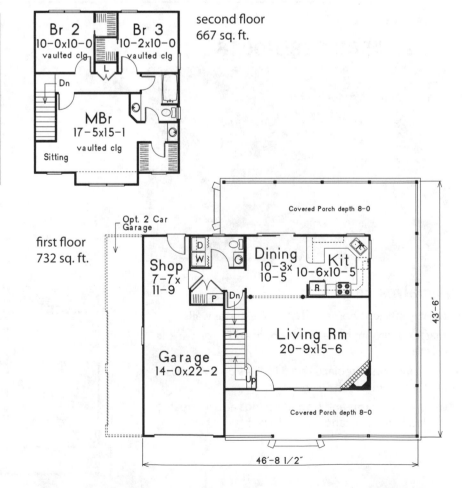

second floor
667 sq. ft.

Br 2
10-0x10-0
vaulted clg

Br 3
10-2x10-0
vaulted clg

Dn

L

MBr
17-5x15-1
vaulted clg

Sitting

first floor
732 sq. ft.

Covered Porch depth 8-0

Opt. 2 Car Garage

Shop
7-7x
11-9

Dining
10-3x
10-5

Kit
10-6x10-5

P

Dn

Living Rm
20-9x15-6

Garage
14-0x22-2

Up

Covered Porch depth 8-0

43'-6"

46'-8 1/2"

plan #588-016D-0030

price code A

plan information

total living area:	1,303
bedrooms:	3
baths:	2
foundation types:	
basement	
crawl space	
slab	
please specify when ordering	

second floor
375 sq. ft.

first floor
928 sq. ft.

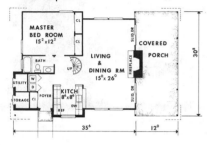

special features

- huge fireplace, surrounded by sliding glass doors, provides easy access to covered porch
- two-story living and dining rooms brightened by skylight and large windows
- a spiral staircase leads to a second floor with two bedrooms successfully sharing a full bath

---

plan #588-047D-0002

price code AA

plan information

total living area:	1,167
bedrooms:	3
baths:	2
garage:	2-car
foundation type:	
slab	

special features

- master suite enjoys a private bath
- the foyer includes a handy coat closet
- lots of storage space throughout

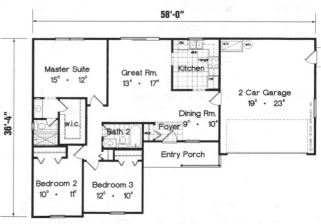

plan #588-040D-0010

price code A

plan information

total living area:	1,496
bedrooms:	3
baths:	2
garage:	2-car drive under
foundation type:	
basement	

special features

- master bedroom features a tray ceiling, walk-in closet and spacious bath
- vaulted ceiling and fireplace grace the family room
- dining room is adjacent to the kitchen and features access to the rear porch
- convenient access to the utility room from the kitchen

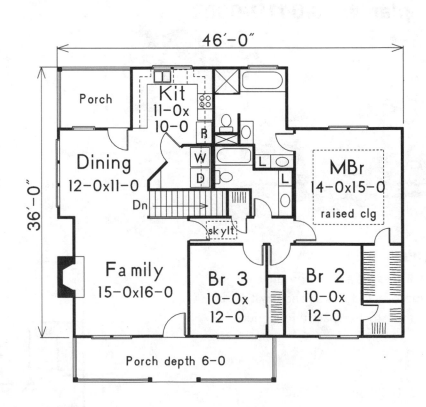

46'-0"

36'-0"

Porch

Kit
11-0x
10-0

Dining
12-0x11-0

Dn

skylt

MBr
14-0x15-0

raised clg

Family
15-0x16-0

Br 3
10-0x
12-0

Br 2
10-0x
12-0

Porch depth 6-0

plan #588-020D-0001

plan information

total living area:	1,375
bedrooms:	3
baths:	2
garage:	2-car carport
foundation type:	
slab	

Width: 61'-0"
Depth: 35'-0"

special features

- master bedroom has a private bath and walk-in closet
- kitchen and dining room are located conveniently near the utility and living rooms
- cathedral ceiling in living room adds spaciousness

---

plan #588-037D-0012

plan information

total living area:	1,661
bedrooms:	3
baths:	2
garage:	2-car
foundation type:	
slab	

special features

- large open foyer with angled wall arrangement and high ceiling adds to spacious living room
- the kitchen and dining area have impressive cathedral ceilings and a French door allowing access to the patio
- utility room is conveniently located near the kitchen
- secluded master bedroom has a large walk-in closet, unique brick wall arrangement and 10' ceiling

plan information

total living area:	1,290
bedrooms:	3
baths:	2
garage:	2-car side entry

foundation types:
- crawl space
- slab
- walk-out basement

please specify when ordering

special features

- the kitchen is located conveniently between the dining room and breakfast area
- master suite has a private luxurious bath with walk-in closet
- decorative plant shelves throughout this plan add style

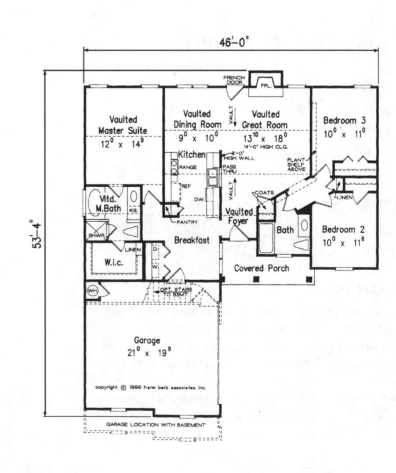

plan #588-053D-0001

price code B

plan information

total living area:	1,582
bedrooms:	3
baths:	2 1/2
garage:	1-car
foundation types:	
slab standard	
crawl space	

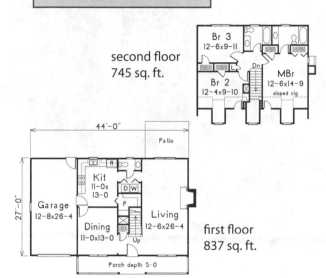

second floor
745 sq. ft.

first floor
837 sq. ft.

special features

- conservative layout gives privacy to living and dining areas
- large fireplace and windows enhance the living area
- rear door in garage is convenient to the garden and kitchen
- full front porch adds charm
- dormers add light to the foyer and bedrooms

---

plan #588-058D-0009

price code AAA

plan information

total living area:	448
bedrooms:	1
baths:	1
foundation type:	
slab	

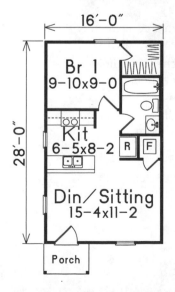

special features

- bedroom features a large walk-in closet ideal for storage
- combined dining/sitting area is ideal for relaxing
- galley-style kitchen is compact and efficient
- covered porch adds to front facade

plan information

total living area:	1,631
bedrooms:	3
baths:	2
garage:	2-car drive under
foundation type:	
basement	

special features

- 9' ceilings throughout this home
- utility room is conveniently located near the kitchen
- roomy kitchen and dining area boast a breakfast bar and deck access
- a raised ceiling accents the master bedroom

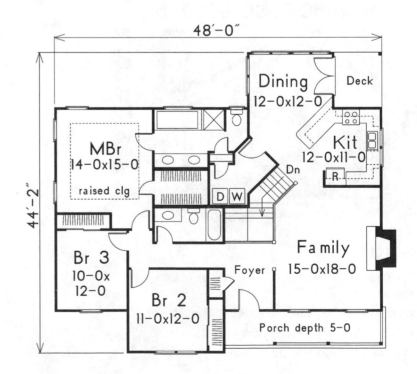

plan #588-032D-0039

price code A

plan information

total living area:	1,288
bedrooms:	2
baths:	1 1/2
garage:	1-car rear entry
foundation type:	
basement	

first floor
691 sq. ft.

second floor
597 sq. ft.

special features

- energy efficient home with 2" x 6" exterior walls
- convenient snack bar in kitchen
- half bath has laundry facilities on first floor
- both second floor bedrooms easily access a full bath

---

plan #588-076D-0013

price code B

plan information

total living area:	1,177
bedrooms:	3
baths:	2
garage:	2-car side entry
foundation type:	
slab	

special features

- the vaulted master bedroom enjoys two walk-in closets, a whirlpool tub and a double vanity
- a grand fireplace flanked by windows graces the spacious family room
- kitchen and breakfast area combine for a relaxing atmosphere and feature access onto the rear patio

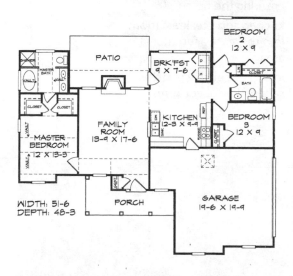

plan #588-039D-0017

price code C

plan information

total living area:	1,966
bedrooms:	3
baths:	2 1/2
garage:	2-car side entry
foundation type:	
basement	

special features

- private dining room remains the focal point when entering the home
- kitchen and breakfast room join to create a functional area
- lots of closet space in the second floor bedrooms

second floor
557 sq. ft.

Attic Storage

Bedroom #3
14 x 12
8' Clg.

Linen

Bedroom #2
13/9 x 11/5
8' Clg.
Sloped Clg.

Width: 48'-2"
Depth: 67'-5"

Garage & Storage
22 x 25/10

Rear Porch
18 x 7/10

Kitchen
11/10 x 10/5

Breakfast
14/3 x 10/5
9' Clg.

Pantry

Stairs Up

Stairs Down

Desk

Family Room
14 x 18/8
9' Clg.

Dining
11 x 11/5
9' Clg.

Master Bedroom
13/9 x 16/8
9' Clg.

Foyer
8/9 x 5/10

first floor
1,409 sq. ft.

Front Porch
40 x 7/10

plan #588-041D-0004

price code AA

plan information

total living area:	1,195
bedrooms:	3
baths:	2
garage:	2-car
foundation type:	
basement	

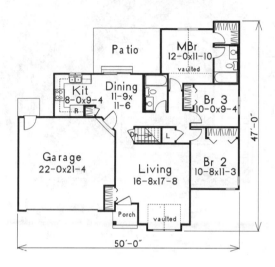

special features

- dining room opens onto the patio
- master bedroom features a vaulted ceiling, private bath and walk-in closet
- coat closets are located by both the entrances
- convenient secondary entrance is located at the back of the garage

---

plan #588-078D-0004

price code D

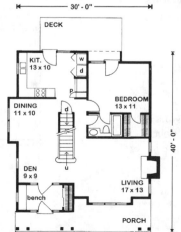

plan information

total living area:	1,425
bedrooms:	3
baths:	2
foundation types:	
crawl space	
basement	
please specify when ordering	

special features

- double-door vestibule entrance features a large closet and window seat
- the living and dining rooms boast vaulted ceilings for added volume and drama
- the kitchen is equipped with a pantry, laundry alcove and French doors opening to a deck

first floor
1,025 sq. ft.

second floor
400 sq. ft.

plan information

total living area:	1,084
bedrooms:	2
baths:	2
foundation type:	
basement	

special features

- delightful country porch for quiet evenings
- the living room offers a front feature window which invites the sun and includes a fireplace and dining area with private patio
- the U-shaped kitchen features lots of cabinets and a bayed breakfast room with built-in pantry
- both bedrooms have walk-in closets and access to their own bath

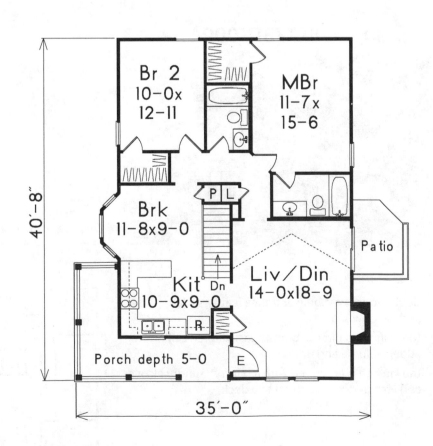

plan #588-029D-0002

price code B

plan information

total living area: 1,619
bedrooms: 3
baths: 3
foundation types:
   basement standard
   crawl space
   slab

special features

- private second floor bedroom and bath
- kitchen features a snack bar and adjacent dining area
- master bedroom has a private bath
- centrally located washer and dryer

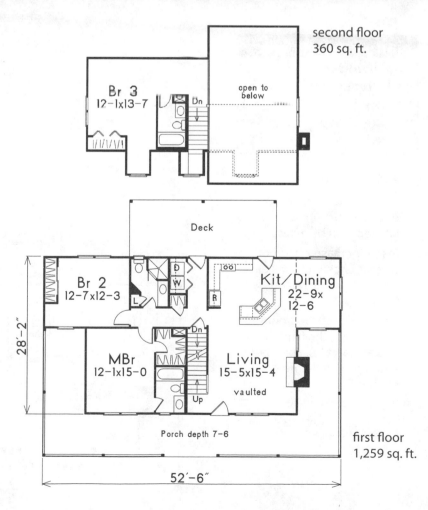

second floor
360 sq. ft.

Br 3
12-1x13-7

open to below

Dn

Deck

Br 2
12-7x12-3

Kit/Dining
22-9x
12-6

MBr
12-1x15-0

Living
15-5x15-4
vaulted

Dn

Up

28'-2"

Porch depth 7-6

52'-6"

first floor
1,259 sq. ft.

plan #588-058D-0020

price code A

plan information

total living area:	1,428
bedrooms:	3
baths:	2
foundation type:	
basement	

special features

- large vaulted family room opens to the dining area and kitchen with breakfast bar

- first floor master bedroom offers a large bath, walk-in closet and nearby laundry facilities

- a spacious loft/bedroom #3 overlooking the family room and an additional bedroom and bath complement the second floor

- 2" x 6" exterior walls available, please order plan #588-058D-0080

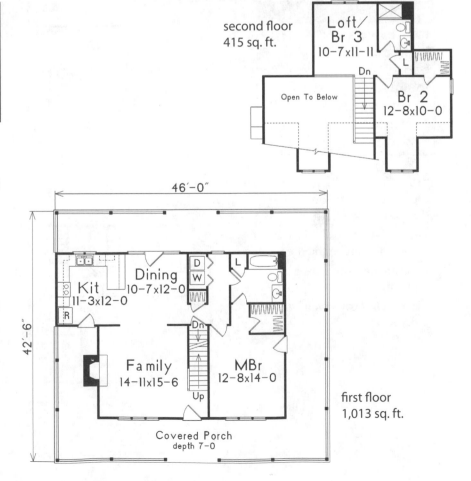

second floor
415 sq. ft.

first floor
1,013 sq. ft.

order 1-800-367-7667

rear view

plan information

total living area:	1,684
bedrooms:	3
baths:	2
garage:	2-car drive under
foundation type:	
walk-out basement	

special features

- delightful wrap-around porch is anchored by a full masonry fireplace

- the vaulted great room includes a large bay window, fireplace, dining balcony and atrium window wall

- double walk-in closets, large luxury bath and sliding doors to an exterior balcony are a few fantastic features of the master bedroom

- atrium opens to 611 square feet of optional living area on the lower level

first floor
1,684 sq. ft.

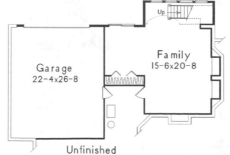

optional
lower level

Unfinished

plan information

total living area:	1,657
bedrooms:	3
baths:	2 1/2
garage:	2-car drive under
foundation type:	
basement	

special features

- stylish pass-through between living and dining areas
- master bedroom is secluded from the living area for privacy
- large windows in the breakfast and dining areas create a bright and cheerful atmosphere

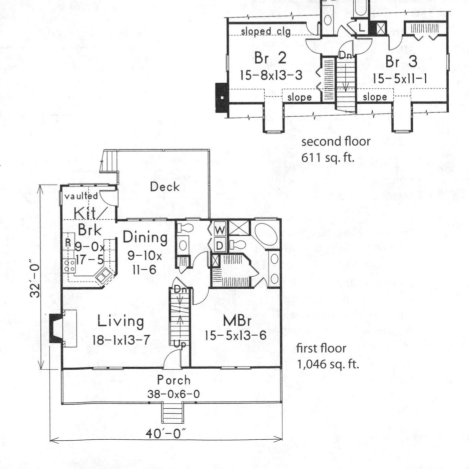

second floor
611 sq. ft.

first floor
1,046 sq. ft.

order 1-800-367-7667

plan information

total living area:	1,320
bedrooms:	3
baths:	2
foundation type:	
crawl space	

special features

- functional U-shaped kitchen features pantry
- large living and dining areas join to create an open atmosphere
- secluded master bedroom includes private full bath
- covered front porch opens into large living area with convenient coat closet
- utility/laundry room is located near the kitchen

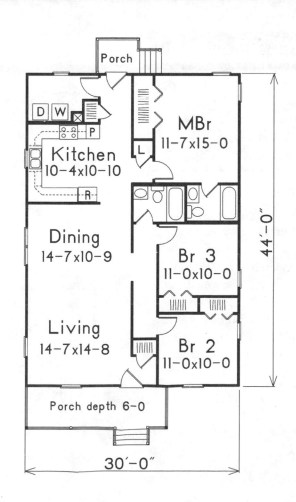

Porch

D W P

Kitchen
10-4x10-10

MBr
11-7x15-0

L

Dining
14-7x10-9

Br 3
11-0x10-0

Living
14-7x14-8

Br 2
11-0x10-0

R

44'-0"

Porch depth 6-0

30'-0"

plan information

total living area:	1,597
bedrooms:	4
baths:	2 1/2
garage:	2-car detached
foundation type:	basement

special features

- spacious family room includes a fireplace and coat closet
- open kitchen and dining room provide a breakfast bar and access to the outdoors
- convenient laundry area is located near the kitchen
- secluded master bedroom enjoys a walk-in closet and private bath

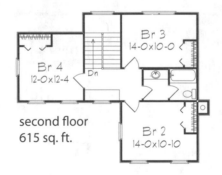

Br 4
12-0x12-4

Br 3
14-0x10-0

Br 2
14-0x10-10

Dn

second floor
615 sq. ft.

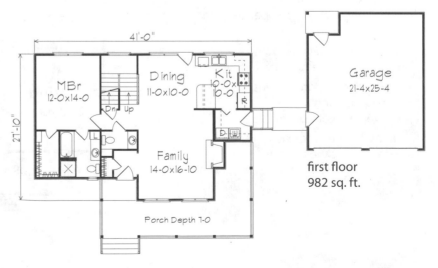

41'-0"

21'-10"

MBr
12-0x14-0

Dn Up

Dining
11-0x10-0

Kit
10-0x10-0

Family
14-0x16-10

Garage
21-4x25-4

first floor
982 sq. ft.

Porch Depth 7-0

plan information

total living area:	1,133
bedrooms:	3
baths:	2
garage:	1-car
foundation type:	
slab	

special features

- this home is designed to fit narrow lots with the main entry on the side
- a U-shaped kitchen includes a breakfast area and porch access
- split bedrooms ensure privacy for the master bedroom suite

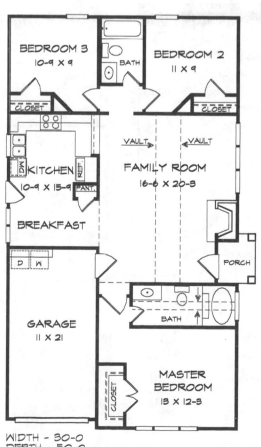

WIDTH - 30-0
DEPTH - 50-0

plan information

total living area:	1,253
bedrooms:	3
baths:	2
garage:	2-car
foundation types:	
crawl space	
slab	
please specify when ordering	

special features

- sloped ceiling and fireplace in family room add drama
- the U-shaped kitchen is efficiently designed
- large walk-in closets are found in all the bedrooms

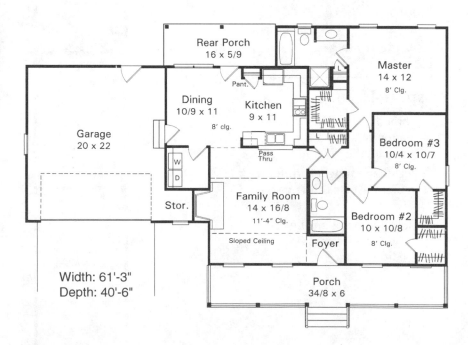

Garage
20 x 22

Rear Porch
16 x 5/9

Pant.

Dining
10/9 x 11
8' clg.

Kitchen
9 x 11

Pass Thru

Master
14 x 12
8' Clg.

Bedroom #3
10/4 x 10/7
8' Clg.

W D

Stor.

Family Room
14 x 16/8
11'-4" Clg.

Sloped Ceiling

Foyer

Bedroom #2
10 x 10/8
8' Clg.

Width: 61'-3"
Depth: 40'-6"

Porch
34/8 x 6

plan #588-013D-0011

plan information

total living area:	1,643
bedrooms:	3
baths:	2 1/2
garage:	2-car drive under

foundation types:
  crawl space
  basement
please specify when ordering

special features

- first floor master bedroom has a private bath, walk-in closet and easy access to the laundry closet
- comfortable family room features a vaulted ceiling and a cozy fireplace
- two bedrooms on the second floor share a bath

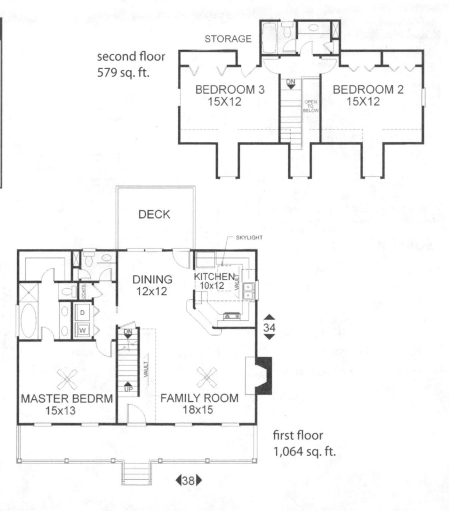

second floor
579 sq. ft.

STORAGE

BEDROOM 3
15X12

BEDROOM 2
15X12

OPEN TO BELOW

DECK

DINING
12x12

KITCHEN
10x12

SKYLIGHT

34

MASTER BEDRM
15x13

FAMILY ROOM
18x15

first floor
1,064 sq. ft.

38

plan #588-016D-0062

price code B

plan information

total living area: 1,380
bedrooms: 3
baths: 2
garage: optional 2-car side entry
foundation types:
  crawl space
  basement
  slab
  please specify when ordering

special features

- built-in bookshelves complement the fireplace in the great room
- an abundance of storage space is near the laundry room and kitchen
- covered porch has a view of the backyard

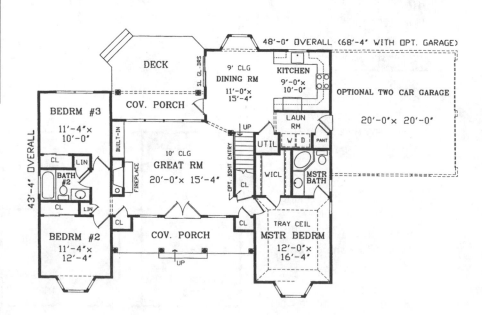

plan #588-022D-0007

plan information

total living area:	1,516
bedrooms:	2
baths:	2 1/2
garage:	2-car
foundation type:	basement

special features

- all living and dining areas are interconnected for a spacious look and easy movement
- covered entrance leads into sunken great room with a rugged corner fireplace
- family kitchen combines practicality with access to other areas
- second floor loft opens to rooms below and can convert to a third bedroom
- the dormer in bedroom #2 adds interest

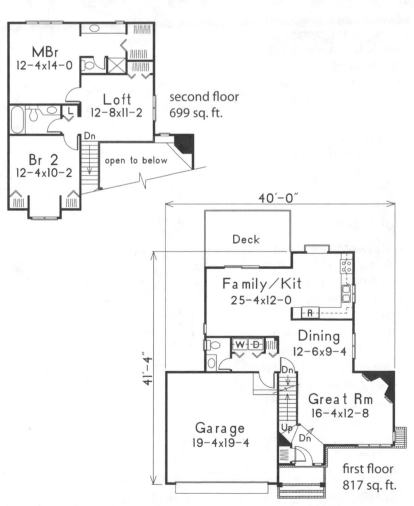

second floor
699 sq. ft.

first floor
817 sq. ft.

plan #588-001D-0024

price code A

plan information

total living area: 1,360
bedrooms: 3
baths: 2
garage: 2-car side entry
foundation types:
   basement standard
   crawl space
   slab

special features

- kitchen/dining room features an island workspace and plenty of dining area
- master bedroom has a large walk-in closet and private bath
- laundry room is adjacent to the kitchen for easy access
- convenient workshop in garage
- large closets in secondary bedrooms maintain organization

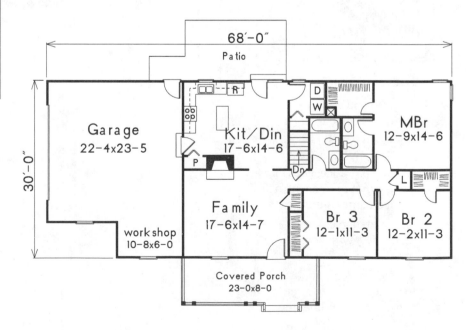

plan information

total living area:	1,539
bedrooms:	3
baths:	2
garage:	2-car carport
foundation types:	
crawl space	
slab	
please specify when ordering	

special features

- the bayed dining room adds style to both the interior and exterior

- a grand fireplace decorates the great room while also warming the adjoining kitchen

- a large laundry area makes this household chore a breeze

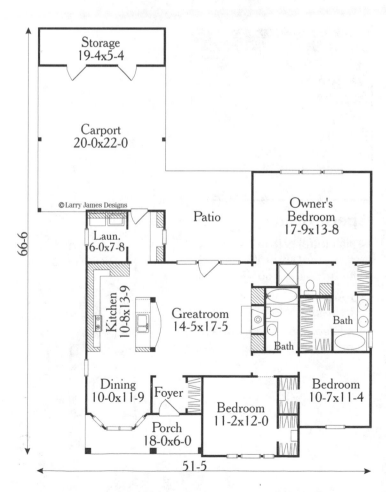

plan #588-007D-0038

price code B

plan information

total living area:	1,524
bedrooms:	3
baths:	2 1/2
garage:	2-car
foundation types:	
basement standard	
crawl space	
slab	

special features

- delightful balcony overlooks two-story entry illuminated by an oval window
- roomy first floor master bedroom offers quiet privacy
- all bedrooms feature one or more walk-in closets

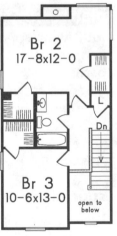

second floor
573 sq. ft.

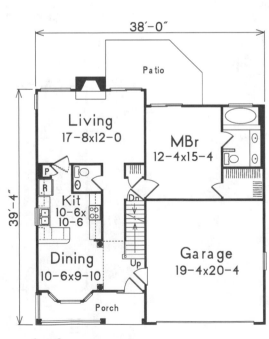

first floor
951 sq. ft.

plan #588-062D-0052

price code B

plan information

total living area:	1,795
bedrooms:	3
baths:	2 1/2

foundation types:
basement
crawl space
please specify when ordering

special features

- energy efficient home with 2" x 6" exterior walls
- window wall in living and dining areas brings the outdoors in
- master bedroom has a full bath and walk-in closet
- vaulted loft on the second floor is a unique feature

first floor
1,157 sq. ft.

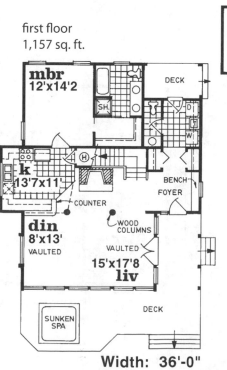

mbr
12'x14'2

SH.

DECK

k
13'7"x11'

H

BENCH

FOYER

COUNTER

din
8'x13'
VAULTED

WOOD COLUMNS

VAULTED

15'x17'8
liv

SUNKEN SPA

DECK

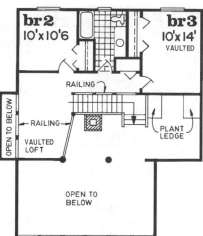

br2
10'x10'6

br3
10'x14'
VAULTED

RAILING

OPEN TO BELOW

RAILING

PLANT LEDGE

VAULTED LOFT

OPEN TO BELOW

second floor
638 sq. ft.

Width: 36'-0"
Depth: 40'-0"

plan information

total living area:	1,140
bedrooms:	3
baths:	2
garage:	2-car drive under
foundation type:	
basement	

special features

- open and spacious living and dining areas for family gatherings
- well-organized kitchen has an abundance of cabinetry and a built-in pantry
- roomy master bath features a double-bowl vanity

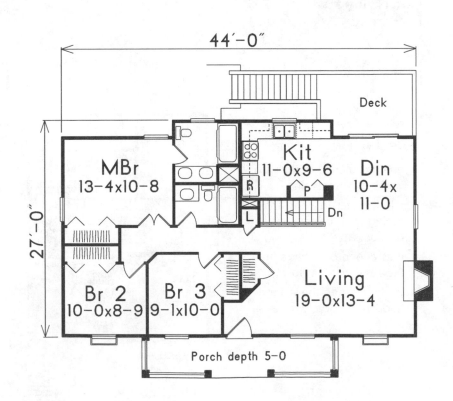

plan #588-008D-0134

plan information

total living area: 1,275
bedrooms: 4
baths: 2
foundation types:
  basement standard
  crawl space
  slab

special features

- wall shingles and stone veneer fireplace all fashion an irresistible rustic appeal
- living area features a fireplace and opens to an efficient kitchen
- two bedrooms on the second floor

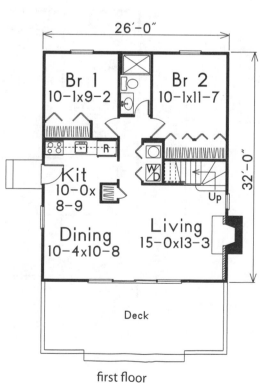

first floor
832 sq. ft.

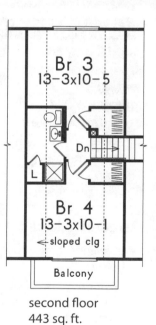

second floor
443 sq. ft.

129

plan #588-028D-0004

price code B

plan information

total living area:	1,785
bedrooms:	3
baths:	3
garage:	2-car detached

foundation types:
  crawl space
  basement
  slab
  please specify when ordering

special features

- 9' ceilings throughout the home
- luxurious master bath includes a whirlpool tub and separate shower
- cozy breakfast area is convenient to the kitchen

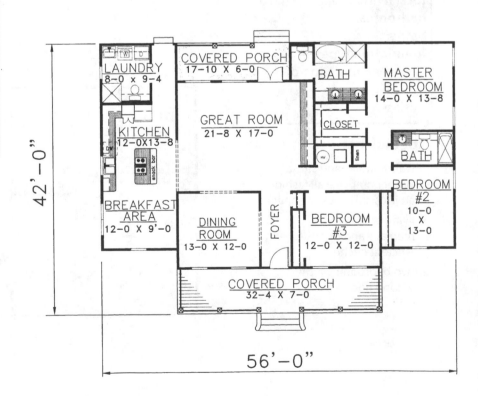

plan #588-016D-0007

plan information

total living area:	1,207
bedrooms:	3
baths:	2

foundation types:
  basement
  crawl space
please specify when ordering

special features

- triple sets of sliding glass doors leading to the deck brighten the living room
- oversized mud room has lots of extra closet space for convenience
- centrally located heat circulating fireplace creates a focal point while warming the home

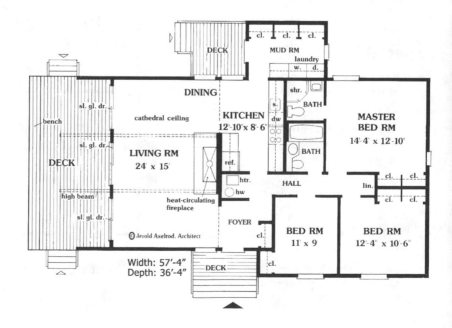

plan #588-058D-0012

price code AA

plan information

total living area:	1,143
bedrooms:	2
baths:	1
foundation type:	
crawl space	

special features

- enormous stone fireplace in the family room adds warmth and character
- spacious kitchen with breakfast bar overlooks the family room
- separate dining area is great for entertaining
- vaulted family room and kitchen create an open atmosphere
- 2" x 6" exterior walls available, please order plan #588-058D-0075

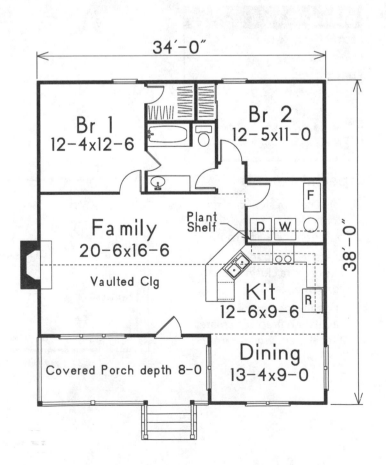

plan #588-078D-0042

price code D

plan information

total living area:	1,280
bedrooms:	3
baths:	2
foundation type:	
crawl space	

special features

- energy efficient home with 2" x 6" exterior walls
- the spacious living room enjoys a cozy bay window and stone fireplace
- the U-shaped kitchen has plenty of counterspace and boasts an attractive bay window behind the sink
- all bedrooms are located on the second floor for added privacy
- one bedroom includes a walk-in closet and private access to a bath making it an ideal master suite

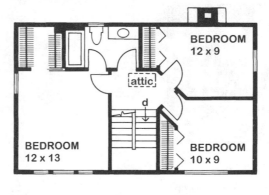

second floor
640 sq. ft.

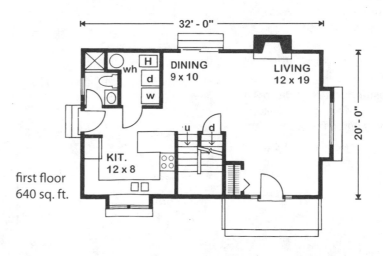

first floor
640 sq. ft.

plan #588-007D-0068

price code B

plan information

total living area:	1,384
bedrooms:	2
baths:	2
garage:	1-car side entry
foundation type:	
walk-out basement	

special features

- wrap-around country porch for peaceful evenings
- vaulted great room enjoys a large bay window, stone fireplace, pass-through kitchen and awesome rear views through an atrium window wall
- master bedroom features a double-door entry, walk-in closet and a fabulous bath
- atrium opens to 611 square feet of optional living area below

optional lower level

Family Rm
25-0x21-4

Patio

Unexcavated

Unfinished Basement

55'-8"

Atrium below

Dn

Dining Area

Kit
10-2x
11-9

Garage
22-0x11-9

Great Rm
18-0x21-8
vaulted

Laundry

D W

46'-0"

Covered porch depth 6-0

Br 2
11-4x12-6

MBr
12-8x15-0

first floor
1,384 sq. ft.

plan information

total living area:	1,668
bedrooms:	3
baths:	2
garage:	2-car drive under
foundation type:	
basement	

special features

- large bay windows grace the breakfast area, master bedroom and dining room
- extensive walk-in closets and storage spaces are located throughout the home
- handy covered entry porch
- large living room has a fireplace, built-in bookshelves and a sloped ceiling

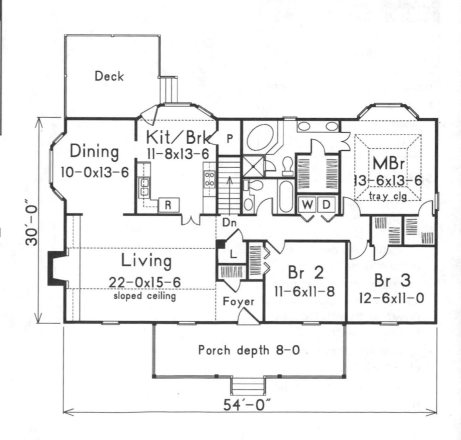

plan information

total living area:	1,393
bedrooms:	3
baths:	2
garage:	2-car detached
foundation types:	
crawl space standard	
slab	

special features

- the L-shaped kitchen features a walk-in pantry, island cooktop and is convenient to the laundry room and dining area
- master bedroom features a large walk-in closet and private bath with separate tub and shower
- convenient storage/coat closet in hall
- view to the patio from the dining area

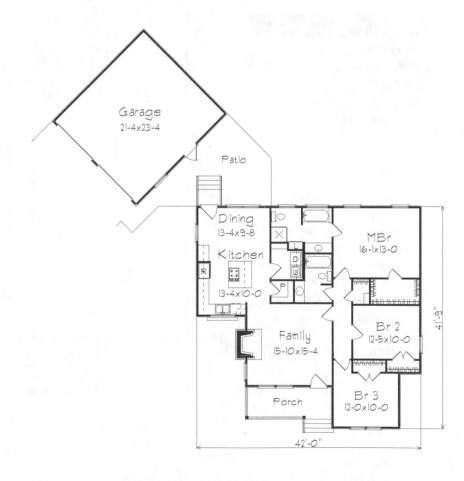

plan information

total living area:	1,501
bedrooms:	3
baths:	2
garage:	2-car side entry

foundation types:
  basement standard
  crawl space
  slab

special features

- spacious kitchen with dining area is open to the outdoors
- convenient utility room is adjacent to the garage
- master bedroom features a private bath, dressing area and access to the large covered porch
- large family room creates openness

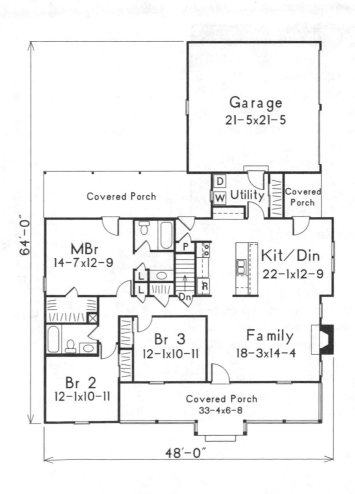

plan information

total living area:	1,830
bedrooms:	3
baths:	2
garage:	3-car side entry

foundation types:

crawl space

basement

slab

please specify when ordering

special features

- inviting covered verandas in the front and rear of the home
- great room has a fireplace and cathedral ceiling
- handy service porch allows easy access
- master bedroom has a vaulted ceiling and private bath

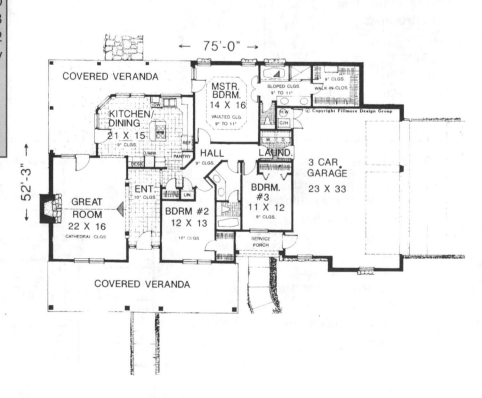

order 1-800-367-7667

plan information

total living area:	1,092
bedrooms:	3
baths:	1 1/2
garage:	1-car
foundation type:	basement

special features

- a box window and inviting porch with dormers create a charming facade
- eat-in kitchen offers a pass-through breakfast bar, corner window wall to patio, pantry and convenient laundry with half bath
- master bedroom features a double-door entry and walk-in closet

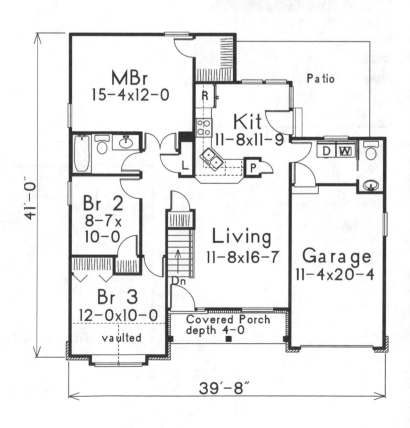

order 1-800-367-7667

plan information

total living area:	1,154
bedrooms:	3
baths:	1 1/2

foundation types:
 crawl space standard
 slab

special features

- the U-shaped kitchen features a large breakfast bar and handy laundry area
- private second floor bedrooms share a half bath
- large living/dining area opens to deck

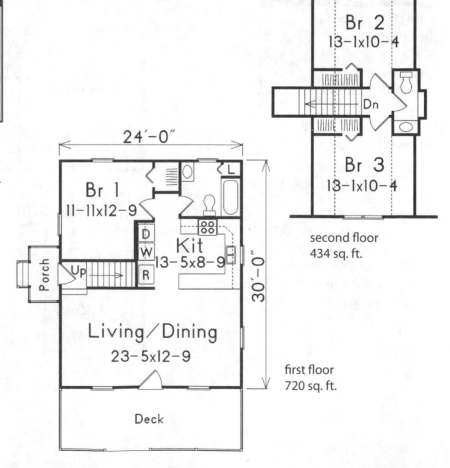

Br 1
11–11x12–9

Up

Porch

D
W
R

Kit
13–5x8–9

L

24'–0"

30'–0"

Living/Dining
23–5x12–9

Deck

first floor
720 sq. ft.

Br 2
13–1x10–4

Dn

Br 3
13–1x10–4

second floor
434 sq. ft.

order 1-800-367-7667

plan information

total living area:	1,170
bedrooms:	3
baths:	2
garage:	2-car
foundation type:	
slab	

special features

- master bedroom enjoys privacy at the rear of this home
- kitchen has an angled bar that overlooks the great room and breakfast area
- living areas combine to create a greater sense of spaciousness
- great room has a cozy fireplace

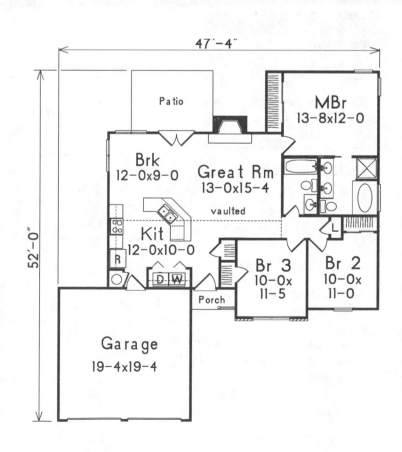

plan information

total living area:	1,368
bedrooms:	3
baths:	2
garage:	2-car
foundation type:	
basement	

special features

- entry foyer steps down to an open living area which combines the great room and formal dining area
- vaulted master bedroom includes a box-bay window and a bath with a large vanity, separate tub and shower
- cozy breakfast area features direct access to the patio and pass-through kitchen
- handy linen closet is located in the hall

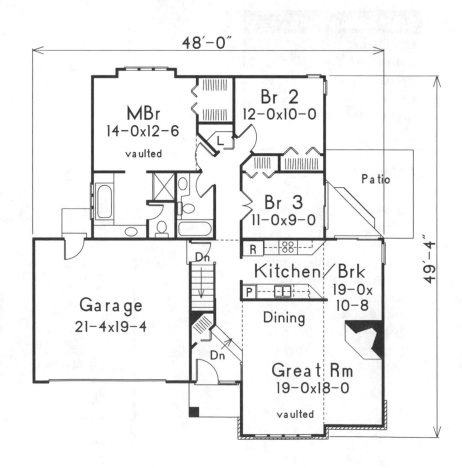

plan #588-080D-0003

plan information

total living area:	1,235
bedrooms:	3
baths:	2
foundation type:	
basement	

special features

- energy efficient home with 2" x 6" exterior walls
- a greenhouse window adorns the kitchen and looks out over the sundeck
- the entire second floor is dedicated to the master bedroom filled with amenities including a private bath and skylights
- abundant skylights and a window wall ensure maximum daylight for the vaulted living and dining rooms

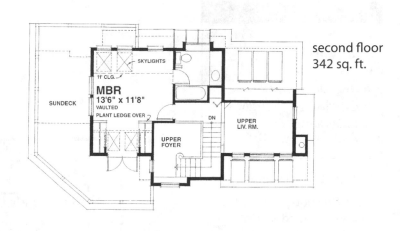

second floor
342 sq. ft.

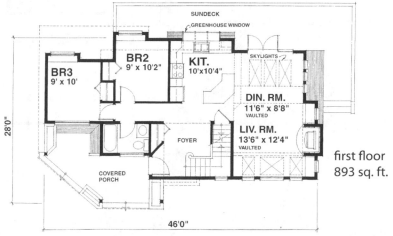

first floor
893 sq. ft.

plan information

total living area:	1,000
bedrooms:	3
baths:	1
foundation types:	
crawl space standard	
basement	
slab	

special features

- bath includes convenient closeted laundry area
- master bedroom includes double closets and private access to the bath
- the foyer features a handy coat closet
- the L-shaped kitchen provides easy access outdoors

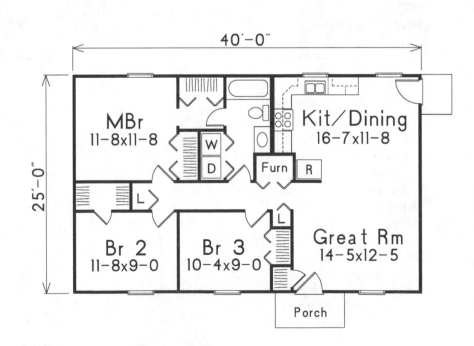

40'-0"

25'-0"

MBr
11-8x11-8

Kit/Dining
16-7x11-8

W
D

Furn   R

L

Br 2
11-8x9-0

Br 3
10-4x9-0

L

Great Rm
14-5x12-5

Porch

plan #588-055D-0013

price code AA

plan information

total living area: 930
bedrooms: 3
baths: 1
foundation types:
slab
crawl space
please specify when ordering

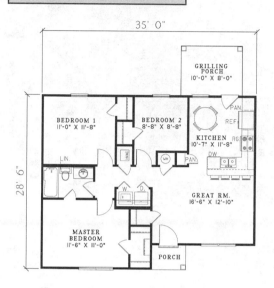

special features

- kitchen overlooks great room and includes space for counter dining
- convenient laundry closet
- master bedroom has walk-in closet and direct access to hall bath

---

plan #588-043D-0008

price code A

special features

- energy efficient home with 2" x 6" exterior walls
- large utility room includes a sink and extra counterspace
- covered patio off the breakfast nook extends dining to the outdoors
- eating counter in the kitchen overlooks the vaulted family room

plan information

total living area: 1,496
bedrooms: 3
baths: 2
garage: 2-car side entry
foundation type:
crawl space

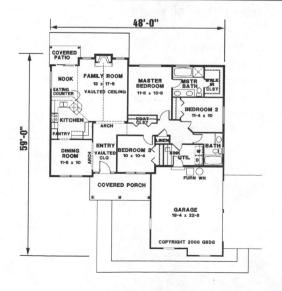

plan #588-040D-0024

price code C

plan information

total living area:	1,874
bedrooms:	4
baths:	2 1/2
garage:	2-car
foundation types:	
basement standard	
slab	

special features

- 9' ceilings throughout the first floor
- two-story foyer opens into the large family room with fireplace
- first floor master bedroom includes a private bath with tub and shower

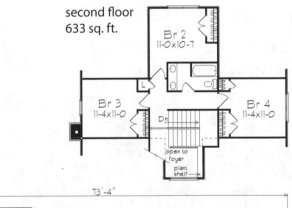

second floor
633 sq. ft.

Br 2
11-0x10-7

Br 3
11-4x11-0

Br 4
11-4x11-0

Dn

open to foyer

plant shelf

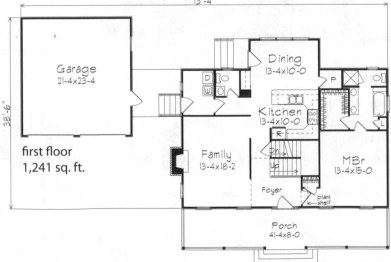

73'-4"

Garage
21-4x23-4

38'-6"

first floor
1,241 sq. ft.

Dining
13-4x10-0

Kitchen
13-4x10-0

Family
13-4x18-2

MBr
13-4x15-0

Foyer

plant shelf

Porch
41-4x8-0

plan #588-001D-0093

price code AA

plan information

total living area:	1,120
bedrooms:	3
baths:	1 1/2
foundation types:	
crawl space standard	
basement	
slab	

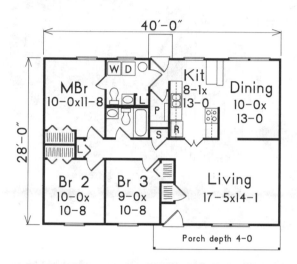

special features

- master bedroom includes a half bath with laundry area, linen closet and kitchen access
- kitchen has charming double-door entry, breakfast bar and a convenient walk-in pantry
- welcoming front porch opens to a large living room with coat closet

---

plan #588-080D-0001

price code AAA

plan information

total living area:	583
bedrooms:	1
baths:	1
foundation type:	
crawl space	

first floor
384 sq. ft.

second floor
199 sq. ft.

special features

- energy efficient home with 2" x 6" exterior walls
- large two-story window wall commands full attention upon entering the living area
- a compact, yet convenient eating bar offers a quick meal option
- the second floor sleeping loft enjoys lots of natural sunlight

147

plan #588-008D-0147

price code A

plan information

total living area:	1,316
bedrooms:	3
baths:	1
foundation type:	
crawl space	

special features

- massive vaulted family/living room is accented with a fireplace and views to the outdoors through sliding glass doors
- galley-style kitchen is centrally located
- unique separate shower room near bath doubles as a convenient mud room

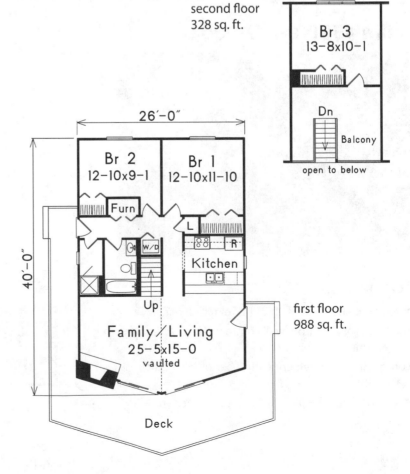

second floor
328 sq. ft.

Br 3
13-8x10-1

Dn

Balcony

open to below

26'-0"

40'-0"

Br 2
12-10x9-1

Furn

Br 1
12-10x11-10

L

W/D

R

Kitchen

Up

Family / Living
25-5x15-0
vaulted

first floor
988 sq. ft.

Deck

plan #588-024D-0003

plan information

total living area:	1,520
bedrooms:	4
baths:	2
foundation type:	
pier	

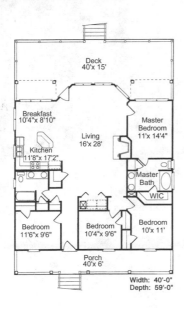

Deck
40'x 15'

Breakfast
10'4"x 8'10"

Living
16'x 28'

Master
Bedroom
11'x 14'4"

Kitchen
11'8"x 17'2"

Master
Bath

WIC

Bedroom
11'6"x 9'6"

Bedroom
10'4"x 9'6"

Bedroom
10'x 11'

Porch
40'x 6'

Width: 40'-0"
Depth: 59'-0"

special features

- 9' ceilings throughout this home
- living room has a fireplace and a large bay window that connects to an oversized deck
- master bedroom has a wall of windows allowing terrific views to the outdoors

---

plan #588-069D-0001

special features

- efficiently designed kitchen/dining are[a] outdoors onto a rear porch
- centrally located laundry closet is conve[nient] part of the home
- future expansion plans included which a[llow] home to become 392 square feet larger [with] bedrooms and 2 baths

special fe[atures]

- second floor m[aster] bedroom is large a sitting area and fe[atures] luxury bath
- 9' ceilings on the first floo[r]
- energy efficient home with 2" x 6" exterior walls
- bonus room on the second floor has an additional 256 square feet of living area

plan information

total living area:	1,760
bedrooms:	3
baths:	2 1/2
garage:	1-car
foundation type:	
basement	

...atures

...aster
...enough for
...atures a

second floor
880 sq. ft.

4,00 X 2,70
13'-4" X 9'-0"

3,30 X 3,30
11'-0" X 11'-0"

BONUS ROOM
4,70 X 4,60
15'-8" X 15'-4"

3,80 X 4,70
12'-8" X 15'-8"

6,20 X 3,40
20'-8" X 11'-4"

5,10 X 3,30
17'-0" X 11'-0"

4,60 X 6,80
15'-4" X 22'-8"

3,80 X 4,70
12'-8" X 15'-8"

first floor
880 sq. ft.

12,6 m
42'-0"

plan #588-007D-0110

price code AA

plan information

total living area:	1,169
bedrooms:	3
baths:	2
garage:	1-car
foundation type:	
basement	

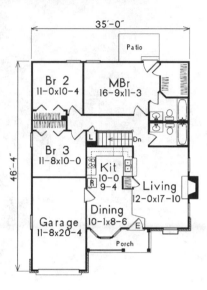

special features

- front facade features a distinctive country appeal
- living room enjoys a wood-burning fireplace and pass-through to kitchen
- a stylish U-shaped kitchen offers an abundance of cabinet and counterspace with view to living room
- a large walk-in closet, access to rear patio and private bath are many features of the master bedroom

---

plan #588-008D-0137

price code A

special features

- expansive deck extends directly off living area
- the L-shaped kitchen is organized and efficient
- bedroom to the left of the kitchen makes a great quiet retreat or office
- living area is flanked with windows for light

plan information

total living area:	1,312
bedrooms:	3
baths:	1
foundation type:	
pier	

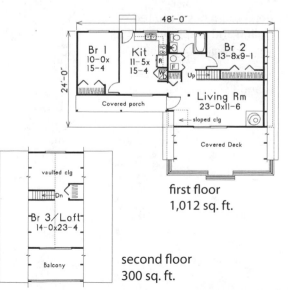

first floor
1,012 sq. ft.

second floor
300 sq. ft.

plan information

total living area:	1,544
bedrooms:	3
baths:	2

foundation types:
- crawl space
- slab

please specify when ordering

special features

- great room has a vaulted ceiling and fireplace
- 32' x 8' grilling porch in rear
- kitchen features a center island

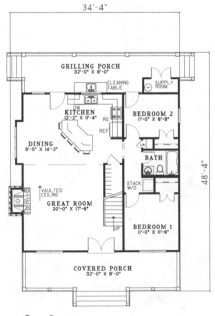

first floor
1,031 sq. ft.

second floor
513 sq. ft.

plan #588-008D-0159

plan information

total living area:	733
bedrooms:	2
baths:	1
foundation type:	
pier	

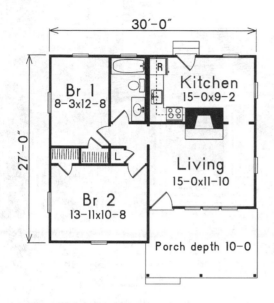

special features

- bedrooms are separate from the kitchen and living area for privacy
- lots of closet space throughout this home
- centrally located bath is easily accessible
- kitchen features a door accessing the outdoors and a door separating it from the rest of the home

---

plan #588-045D-0019

plan information

total living area:	1,134
bedrooms:	2
baths:	1
garage:	2-car
foundation type:	
basement	

special features

- kitchen has plenty of counterspace, an island worktop, large pantry and access to the garage
- living room features a vaulted ceiling, fireplace and access to an expansive patio
- bedroom #1 has a large walk-in closet
- convenient linen closet in the hall

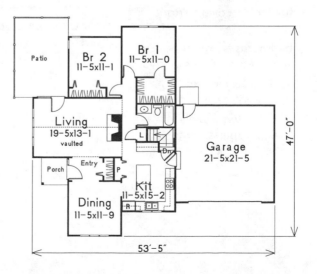

plan information

total living area:	1,000
bedrooms:	2
baths:	1
foundation type:	
crawl space	

special features

- large mud room has a separate covered porch entrance
- full-length covered front porch
- bedrooms are on opposite sides of the home for privacy
- vaulted ceiling creates an open and spacious feeling
- 2" x 6" exterior walls available, please order plan #588-058D-0085

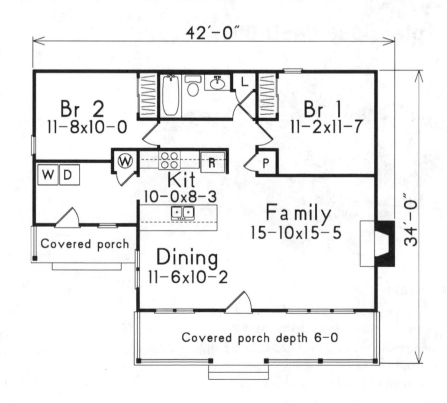

42'-0"

34'-0"

Br 2
11-8x10-0

Br 1
11-2x11-7

W D

Kit
10-0x8-3

P

Covered porch

Family
15-10x15-5

Dining
11-6x10-2

Covered porch depth 6-0

plan #588-020D-0014

price code AA

plan information

total living area:	1,150
bedrooms:	2
baths:	2
garage:	2-car
foundation types:	
slab standard	
crawl space	

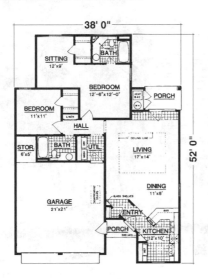

special features

- bedroom with attached sitting area would make a nice master bedroom
- living and dining rooms have 11' high box ceilings
- ornate trimwork accents the wood sided exterior

---

plan #588-040D-0015

price code B

plan information

total living area:	1,655
bedrooms:	3
baths:	2
garage:	2-car
foundation type:	
crawl space	

special features

- master bedroom features a 9' ceiling, walk-in closet and bath with dressing area
- oversized family room includes a 10' ceiling and masonry see-through fireplace
- island kitchen has convenient access to the laundry room
- handy covered walkway from the garage leads to the kitchen and dining area

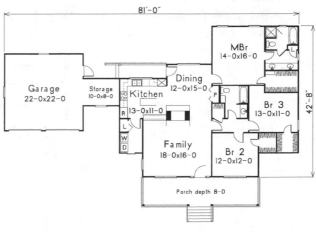

plan #588-045D-0018

price code AAA

plan information

total living area:	858
bedrooms:	2
baths:	1
foundation type:	
crawl space	

special features

- stackable washer/dryer is located in the kitchen
- large covered porch graces this exterior
- both bedrooms have walk-in closets

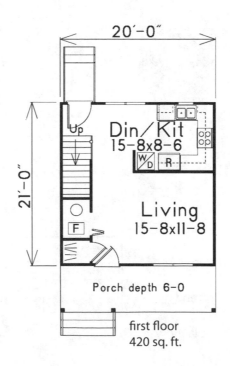

20'-0"

21'-0"

Up

Din/Kit
15-8x8-6

W/D   R

F

Living
15-8x11-8

Porch depth 6-0

first floor
420 sq. ft.

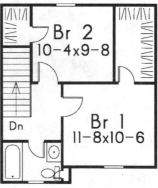

second floor
438 sq. ft.

Br 2
10-4x9-8

Dn

Br 1
11-8x10-6

plan #588-039D-0005

price code A

plan information

total living area:	1,474
bedrooms:	3
baths:	2
garage:	2-car detached
foundation types:	
slab	
crawl space	
please specify when ordering	

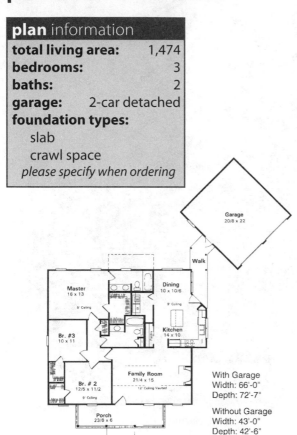

With Garage
Width: 66'-0"
Depth: 72'-7"

Without Garage
Width: 43'-0"
Depth: 42'-6"

special features

- kitchen and dining area include center eat-in island and large pantry
- laundry facilities and hall bath are roomy
- both secondary bedrooms have walk-in closets

---

plan #588-022D-0022

price code A

special features

- spacious living area features angled stairs, vaulted ceiling, exciting fireplace and deck access
- master bedroom includes a walk-in closet and private bath
- dining and living rooms join to create an open atmosphere
- eat-in kitchen has a convenient pass-through to dining room

plan information

total living area:	1,270
bedrooms:	3
baths:	2
garage:	2-car
foundation type:	
basement	

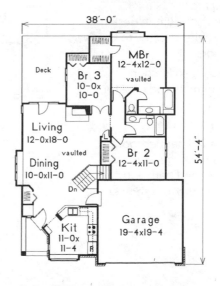

plan #588-040D-0014

price code B

plan information

total living area:	1,595
bedrooms:	3
baths:	2
garage:	2-car side entry
foundation types:	
slab standard	
crawl space	

special features

- dining room has a convenient built-in desk and provides access to the outdoors
- the L-shaped kitchen features an island cooktop
- family room has a high ceiling and fireplace
- private master bedroom includes a large walk-in closet and bath with separate tub and shower units

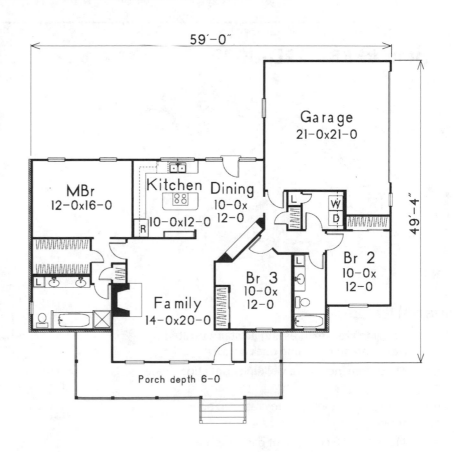

59'-0"

49'-4"

Garage
21-0x21-0

MBr
12-0x16-0

Kitchen
10-0x12-0

Dining
10-0x
12-0

R

L

W
D

Br 2
10-0x
12-0

L

Br 3
10-0x
12-0

Family
14-0x20-0

Porch depth 6-0

plan #588-058D-0043

price code A

plan information

total living area:	1,277
bedrooms:	3
baths:	2
garage:	2-car
foundation type:	
basement	

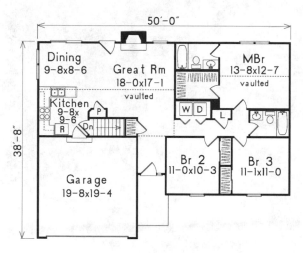

special features

- energy efficient home with 2" x 6" exterior walls
- vaulted ceilings grace the master bedroom, great room, kitchen and dining room
- laundry closet is located near the bedrooms for convenience
- compact, yet efficient kitchen

---

plan #588-076D-0162

price code A

plan information

total living area:	1,458
bedrooms:	3
baths:	2
garage:	2-car
foundation types:	
crawl space	
slab	
please specify when ordering	

special features

- the vaulted foyer leads to the back of the home where you will find a massive family room and adjoined dining area
- the chef of the family will enjoy the efficient kitchen with wrap-around counter with seating that opens to the rear yard
- it will be easy to relax in this master suite that features a decorative ceiling and a lavish private bath
- the optional second floor has an additional 256 square feet of living area

first floor
1,458 sq. ft.

optional second floor

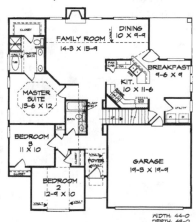

order 1-800-367-7667

plan information

total living area:	1,574
bedrooms:	3
baths:	2
foundation type:	
basement	

special features

- energy efficient home with 2" x 6" exterior walls
- secluded bedroom on first floor has plenty of privacy
- lower level includes another living area in addition to the secondary bedrooms

first floor
787 sq. ft.

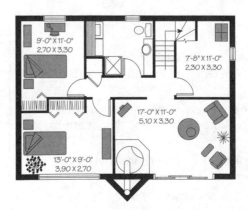

lower level
787 sq. ft.

plan #588-008D-0162

price code AAA

plan information

total living area:	865
bedrooms:	2
baths:	1
foundation type:	
pier	

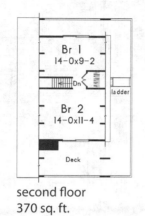

first floor
495 sq. ft.

second floor
370 sq. ft.

special features

- central living area provides an enormous amount of space for gathering around the fireplace
- the outdoor ladder on the wrap-around deck connects the top deck with the main deck
- kitchen is bright and cheerful with lots of windows and access to the deck

---

plan #588-058D-0031

price code AA

plan information

total living area:	990
bedrooms:	2
baths:	1
foundation type:	
crawl space	

special features

- covered front porch adds a charming feel
- vaulted ceilings in the kitchen, family and dining rooms create a spacious feel
- large linen, pantry and storage closets throughout

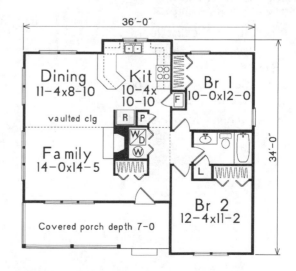

plan information

total living area:	2,202
bedrooms:	5
baths:	3 full, 3 half
garage:	2-car drive under
foundation type:	
walk-out basement	

special features

- energy efficient home with 2" x 6" exterior walls
- 9' ceilings on the first floor
- guest bedroom located on the first floor for convenience could easily be converted to an office area
- large kitchen with oversized island overlooks dining area

Width: 34'-0"   Depth: 46'-0"

first floor
1,174 sq. ft.

second floor
1,028 sq. ft.

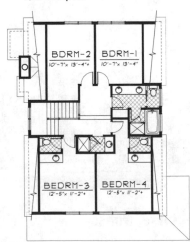

plan #588-058D-0003

price code AA

plan information

total living area:	1,020
bedrooms:	2
baths:	1
foundation type:	
slab	

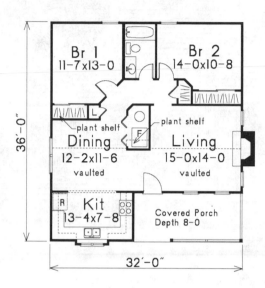

Br 1
11-7x13-0

Br 2
14-0x10-8

plant shelf

plant shelf

Dining
12-2x11-6
vaulted

Living
15-0x14-0
vaulted

Kit
13-4x7-8

Covered Porch
Depth 8-0

36'-0"

32'-0"

special features

- living room is warmed by a fireplace
- dining and living rooms are enhanced by vaulted ceilings and plant shelves
- the U-shaped kitchen features a large window over the sink

---

plan #588-062D-0030

price code A

plan information

total living area:	1,293
bedrooms:	2
baths:	1
garage:	1-car carport
foundation type:	
crawl space	

special features

- compact kitchen includes snack counter for convenience
- both bedrooms have sliding glass doors leading to a spacious sundeck
- vaulted living area is sunny and bright with double sliding glass doors accessing the outdoors

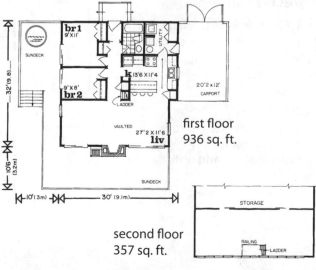

br1
9'X11'

SUNDECK

UTILITY

br2
9'X8'

k 13'6 X 11'4

LADDER

20'2 x12'
CARPORT

VAULTED

27'2 X 11'6
liv

SUNDECK

32'(9.8)

10'6(3.2m)

10'(3m)

30' (9.1m)

first floor
936 sq. ft.

STORAGE

RAILING

LADDER

second floor
357 sq. ft.

plan #588-084D-0016

price code C

rear view

plan information

total living area:	1,492
bedrooms:	3
baths:	2
garage:	2-car side entry

foundation types:
  crawl space
  basement
  slab
  please specify when ordering

special features

- high ceilings increase the spaciousness of this design
- the kitchen and dining area combine with a handy island snack bar and access to the rear porch
- a private master bedroom enjoys a deluxe bath with whirlpool tub and walk-in closet

Width 56-0

Porch
31-4x7-8
9' ceiling

Bedroom
11-4x11-4
9' ceiling

Kitchen/Dining
19-11x11-4
9' ceiling

Snack Bar

Master Bedroom
16-6x13-2
9' ceiling

Closet
6-6x8-0

Shlvs

Laundry
6-7x5-10

M.Bath
12-4x11-0
9' ceiling

Bath

Shlvs

Greatroom
16-11x19-0
11' ceiling

Storage

Garage
21-3x19-2
9' ceiling

Bedroom
11-4x11-4
9' Ceiling

Depth 45-8

Porch
32-0x5-4
9' ceiling

©Larry James Designs

plan #588-080D-0004

price code AA

plan information

total living area:	1,154
bedrooms:	2
baths:	2
foundation type:	
crawl space	

first floor
672 sq. ft.

second floor
482 sq. ft.

special features

- energy efficient home with 2" x 6" exterior walls
- the multi-purpose vaulted great room is up to the challenges of evolving cottage activities
- designed for relaxed living, this design enjoys access all around onto the large deck
- a wrap-around window seat in the living/dining room is a cozy place to curl up with a book
- the second floor studio would make a perfect artist's retreat, a home office or private escape perfect for taking in views on the balcony

---

plan #588-069D-0006

price code A

plan information

total living area:	1,277
bedrooms:	3
baths:	2
foundation types:	
slab	
crawl space	
please specify when ordering	

special features

- expansive great room features an 11' vaulted ceiling, cozy fireplace and coat closet
- utility room, kitchen and dining area combine for an open atmosphere
- master bedroom is located away from the secondary bedrooms for privacy

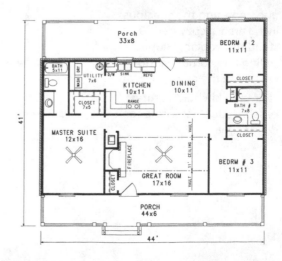

plan #588-008D-0148

price code AAA

plan information

total living area:	784
bedrooms:	3
baths:	1
foundation type:	
pier	

special features

- outdoor relaxation will be enjoyed with this home's huge wrap-around wood deck

- upon entering the spacious living area, a cozy free-standing fireplace, sloped ceiling and corner window wall catch the eye

- charming kitchen features pass-through peninsula to dining area

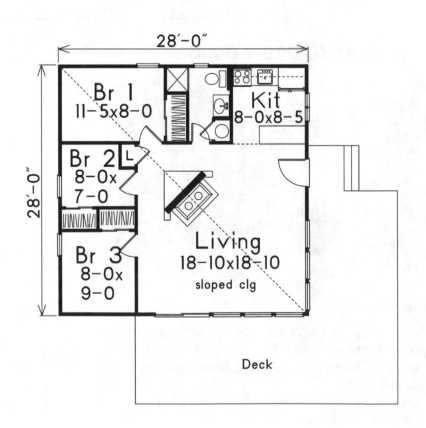

28'-0"

28'-0"

Br 1
11-5x8-0

Kit
8-0x8-5

Br 2
8-0x
7-0

Br 3
8-0x
9-0

Living
18-10x18-10
sloped clg

Deck

plan #588-022D-0024

price code AA

plan information

total living area:	1,127
bedrooms:	2
baths:	2
garage:	2-car
foundation type:	
basement	

special features

- plant shelf joins kitchen and dining room
- vaulted master bedroom has double walk-in closets, deck access and a private bath
- great room features a vaulted ceiling, fireplace and sliding doors to the covered deck
- ideal home for a narrow lot

---

plan #588-060D-0022

price code A

plan information

total living area:	1,436
bedrooms:	3
baths:	2
garage:	2-car
foundation type:	
slab	

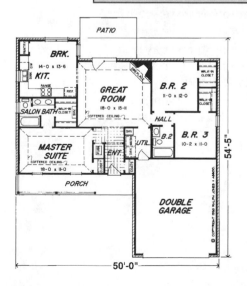

special features

- corner fireplace in the great room warms home
- kitchen and breakfast area combine for convenience
- centrally located utility room

order 1-800-367-7667

plan information

total living area:	1,167
bedrooms:	2
baths:	1
foundation type:	
crawl space	

special features

- energy efficient home with 2" x 6" exterior walls

- bedrooms are separate for privacy

- unique observatory is perfect for mountain, lake or seaside views

- second floor bedroom includes a large sitting area

second floor
345 sq. ft.

observatory

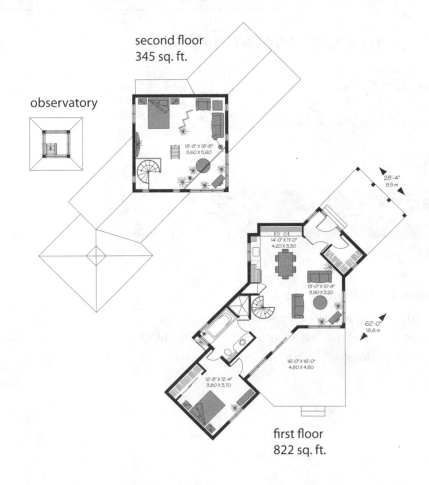

first floor
822 sq. ft.

plan #588-008D-0138

price code A

plan information

total living area: 1,280
bedrooms: 4
baths: 2
foundation types:
  crawl space standard
  basement

first floor
832 sq. ft.

second floor
448 sq. ft.

special features

- attention to architectural detail has created the look of an authentic Swiss cottage
- spacious living room, adjacent kitchenette and dining area all enjoy views to the front deck
- hall bath shared by two sizable bedrooms is included on the first and second floors

---

plan #588-078D-0149

price code D

plan information

total living area: 1,540
bedrooms: 3
baths: 2
foundation type:
  basement

first floor
910 sq. ft.

second floor
630 sq. ft.

special features

- large front porch welcomes guests into this unique two-story home
- the kitchen/dining area combines with the living room for a spacious atmosphere and are warmed by the grand fireplace
- secondary bedrooms share a full bath and comprise the second floor

plan information

total living area:	828
bedrooms:	2
baths:	1
foundation type:	
crawl space	

special features

- vaulted ceiling in living area enhances space
- convenient laundry room
- sloped ceiling creates unique style in bedroom #2
- efficient storage space under the stairs
- covered entry porch provides a cozy sitting area and plenty of shade

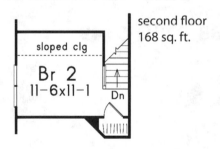

second floor
168 sq. ft.

sloped clg

Br 2
11-6x11-1

Dn

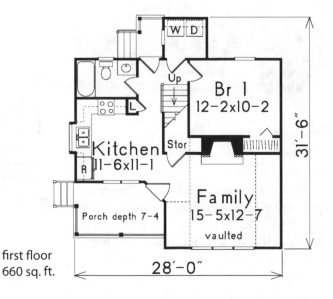

W D

Up

Br 1
12-2x10-2

Kitchen
11-6x11-1

Stor

Family
15-5x12-7

vaulted

Porch depth 7-4

31'-6"

28'-0"

first floor
660 sq. ft.

plan #588-058D-0008

price code A

plan information

total living area:	1,285
bedrooms:	2
baths:	1
foundation type:	
crawl space	

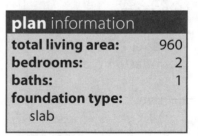

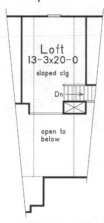

second floor
253 sq. ft.

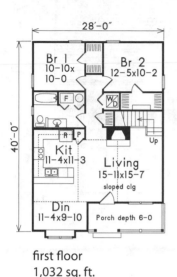

first floor
1,032 sq. ft.

special features

- dining nook creates a warm feeling with sunny box-bay window
- second floor loft is perfect for a recreation space or office hideaway
- bedrooms include walk-in closets allowing extra storage space
- kitchen, dining and living areas combine making a perfect gathering place

---

plan #588-015D-0009

price code AA

plan information

total living area:	960
bedrooms:	2
baths:	1
foundation type:	
slab	

special features

- energy efficient home with 2" x 6" exterior walls
- cozy, yet open floor plan is perfect for a vacation getaway or a guest house
- spacious kitchen features peninsula cooktop with breakfast bar that overlooks the large living room
- bath is complete with laundry facilities
- front deck is ideal for enjoying views or outdoor entertaining

plan #588-060D-0029

price code A

plan information

total living area:	1,270
bedrooms:	3
baths:	2
garage:	1-car
foundation types:	
crawl space	
slab	
please specify when ordering	

special features

- convenient master suite on the first floor
- two secondary bedrooms on the second floor each have a large walk-in closet and share a full bath
- sunny breakfast room has lots of sunlight and easy access to the great room and kitchen

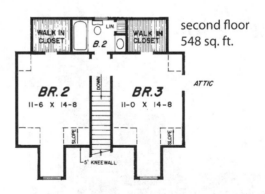

second floor
548 sq. ft.

first floor
722 sq. ft.

plan #588-032D-0016

price code AA

plan information

total living area:	1,120
bedrooms:	2
baths:	1 1/2
foundation type:	
slab	

first floor
587 sq. ft.

24'-0"
7.2 m

26'-0"
8.0 m

second floor
533 sq. ft.

special features

- energy efficient home with 2" x 6" exterior walls
- dining and cooking island in kitchen makes food preparation easy
- all bedrooms on second floor for privacy from living area
- convenient laundry closet on first floor

---

plan #588-001D-0060

price code C

plan information

total living area:	1,818
bedrooms:	3
baths:	2 1/2
garage:	1-car carport
foundation types:	
crawl space standard	
basement	
slab	

special features

- spacious living and dining rooms
- master bedroom has a walk-in closet, dressing area and bath
- convenient carport and storage area

second floor
890 sq. ft.

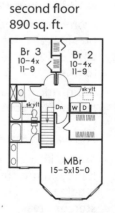

first floor
928 sq. ft.

plan #588-021D-0008

price code A

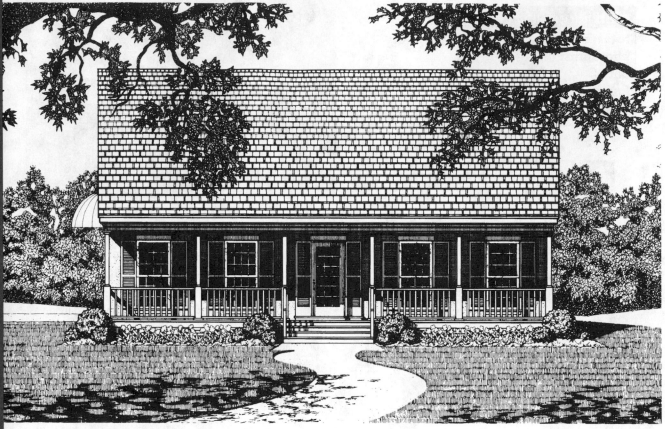

plan information

total living area:	1,266
bedrooms:	3
baths:	2
garage:	2-car rear entry
foundation types:	
crawl space standard	
slab	

special features

- narrow frontage is perfect for small lots
- energy efficient home with 2" x 6" exterior walls
- prominent central hall provides a convenient connection for all main rooms
- design incorporates full-size master bedroom complete with dressing room, bath and walk-in closet
- angled kitchen includes handy laundry facilities and is adjacent to an oversized storage area

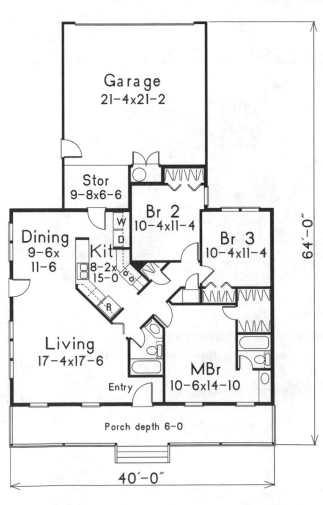

Garage
21-4x21-2

Stor
9-8x6-6

Br 2
10-4x11-4

Br 3
10-4x11-4

Dining
9-6x
11-6

Kit
8-2x
15-0

Living
17-4x17-6

MBr
10-6x14-10

Entry

Porch depth 6-0

64'-0"

40'-0"

plan #588-032D-0041

price code A

plan information

total living area: 1,482
bedrooms: 2
baths: 1 1/2
foundation type:
  basement

second floor
587 sq. ft.

first floor
895 sq. ft.

special features

- energy efficient home with 2" x 6" exterior walls
- corner fireplace warms living area
- screened porch is spacious and connects to main living area in the home
- two bedrooms on the second floor share a spacious bath

---

plan #588-080D-0005

price code A

plan information

total living area: 1,333
bedrooms: 2
baths: 2
foundation type:
  crawl space

special features

- energy efficient home with 2" x 6" exterior walls
- vaulted ceiling and a woodstove create a warm, yet spacious feeling to the great room
- the second floor studio has an appealing open railing looking down to the great room
- a private bedroom and bath complete the second floor

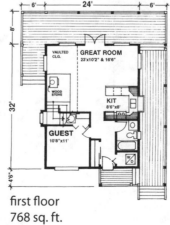

first floor
768 sq. ft.

second floor
565 sq. ft.

175

plan #588-060D-0012

price code AA

plan information

total living area:	977
bedrooms:	3
baths:	2
garage:	optional 1-car
foundation types:	
slab	
crawl space	
please specify when ordering	

special features

- large storage closet ideal for patio furniture storage or lawn equipment
- large kitchen with enough room for dining looks into oversized living room
- front covered porch adds charm

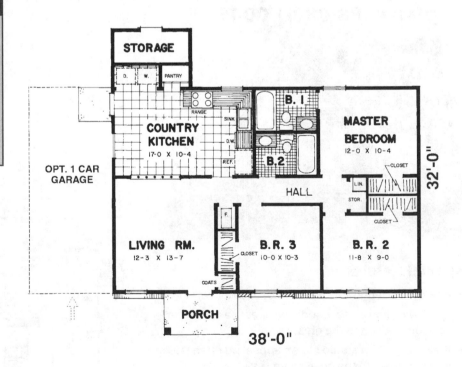

plan #588-032D-0008

price code AA

plan information

total living area:	1,106
bedrooms:	3
baths:	1
foundation type:	
basement	

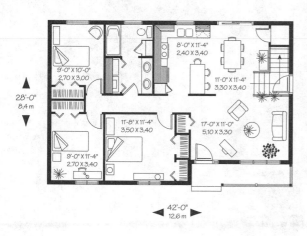

28'-0"
8,4 m

42'-0"
12,6 m

special features

- energy efficient home with 2" x 6" exterior walls
- kitchen has additional counterspace for dining
- well-organized bath includes laundry closet
- dining area has access to the outdoors through sliding glass doors

---

plan #588-007D-0032

price code A

plan information

total living area:	1,294
bedrooms:	2
baths:	1 full, 2 half
garage:	1-car rear entry
foundation type:	
basement	

special features

- great room features a fireplace and large bay with windows and patio doors
- enjoy a laundry room immersed in light with large windows, an arched transom and attractive planter box
- vaulted master bedroom features a bay window and two walk-in closets
- bedroom #2 boasts a vaulted ceiling, plant shelf and half bath, perfect for a studio

first floor
718 sq. ft.

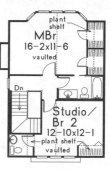

second floor
576 sq. ft.

plan information

total living area:	1,516
bedrooms:	3
baths:	2
foundation type:	
basement	

special features

- energy efficient home with 2" x 6" exterior walls
- warm fireplace adds coziness to living areas
- dining area and kitchen are convenient to each other making entertaining easy

second floor
454 sq. ft.

first floor
1,062 sq. ft.

plan #588-028D-0006

plan information

total living area:	1,700
bedrooms:	3
baths:	2
foundation types:	
crawl space	
slab	
please specify when ordering	

price code B

50-0 WIDE X 42-0 DEEP
(INCLUDING COVERED PORCH)

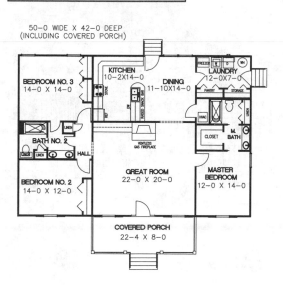

special features

- oversized laundry room has a large pantry and storage area as well as access to the outdoors
- master bedroom is separated from other bedrooms for privacy
- raised snack bar in kitchen allows extra seating for dining

---

plan #588-008D-0145

special features

- the family room is brightened by floor-to-ceiling windows and sliding doors providing access to a large deck
- second floor sitting area is perfect for a game room or entertaining
- kitchen includes eat-in dining area plus outdoor dining patio as a bonus
- plenty of closet and storage space throughout

price code B

plan information

total living area:	1,750
bedrooms:	3
baths:	2
foundation types:	
basement standard	
crawl space	
slab	

first floor
1,126 sq. ft.

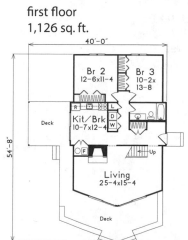

second floor
624 sq. ft.

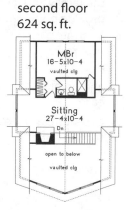

plan #588-078D-0020

plan information

total living area:	1,700
bedrooms:	3
baths:	2 1/2
foundation types:	
basement	
crawl space	
please specify when ordering	

special features

- energy efficient home with 2" x 6" exterior walls
- the family and living rooms provide both formal and informal gathering areas
- the U-shaped kitchen serves the adjoining dining room and breakfast nook with ease
- bedrooms are located on the second floor for privacy

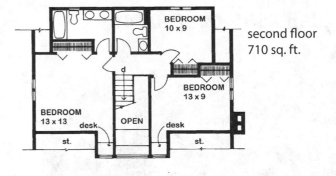

second floor
710 sq. ft.

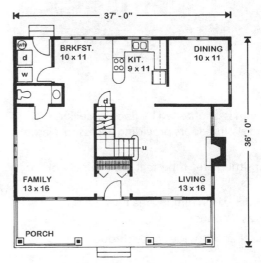

first floor
990 sq. ft.

plan #588-062D-0033

plan information

total living area:	1,286
bedrooms:	3
baths:	2
foundation type:	
crawl space	

price code A

first floor
725 sq. ft.

Width: 25'-0"
Depth: 36'-6"

second floor
561 sq. ft.

special features

- energy efficient home with 2" x 6" exterior walls
- living room has a warm fireplace and a dining room with a snack bar counter through to the kitchen
- the U-shaped kitchen has a window sink
- the master bedroom has private access to a balcony
- lots of storage throughout this home

plan #588-032D-0009

special features

- energy efficient home with 2" x 6" exterior walls
- open living spaces are ideal for entertaining
- spacious kitchen has lots of extra counterspace
- nice-sized bedrooms are separated by a full bath

price code AA

plan information

total living area:	1,199
bedrooms:	2
baths:	1
foundation type:	
basement	

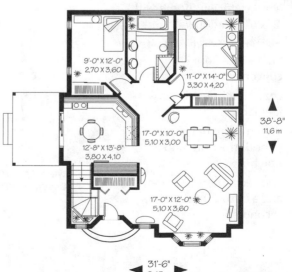

plan #588-062D-0059

price code B

plan information

total living area: 1,588
bedrooms: 3
baths: 2 1/2
foundation types:
  basement
  crawl space
  please specify when ordering

special features

- energy efficient home with 2" x 6" exterior walls
- master bedroom is located on the first floor for convenience
- cozy great room has a fireplace
- dining room has access to both the front and rear porches
- two secondary bedrooms and a bath complete the second floor

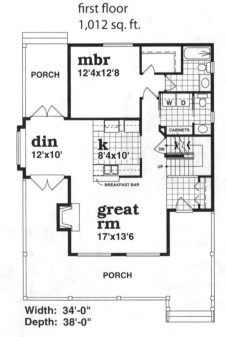

first floor
1,012 sq. ft.

PORCH

mbr
12'4x12'8

W D

CABINETS

din
12'x10'

k
8'4x10'

DN

UP

BREAKFAST BAR

great rm
17'x13'6

PORCH

Width: 34'-0"
Depth: 38'-0"

br2
12'4x12'8

br3
10'x10'
OR OPTIONAL LOFT

DN

3'6 RAILING

OPEN TO BELOW

second floor
576 sq. ft.

plan #588-032D-0010

plan information

total living area: 1,066
bedrooms: 2
baths: 1
foundation type:
  basement

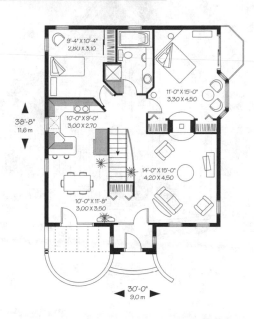

price code AA

special features

- energy efficient home with 2" x 6" exterior walls
- separate front hall with closet makes an interesting entrance
- family room has see-through fireplace which it shares with the master bedroom
- dining area has access to outdoor balcony/patio

---

plan #588-058D-0030

special features

- wrap-around porch creates a relaxing retreat
- combined family and dining rooms boast a vaulted ceiling
- space for an efficiency washer and dryer unit offers convenience
- 2" x 6" exterior walls available, please order plan #588-058D-0086

price code AA

plan information

total living area: 990
bedrooms: 2
baths: 1
foundation type:
  crawl space

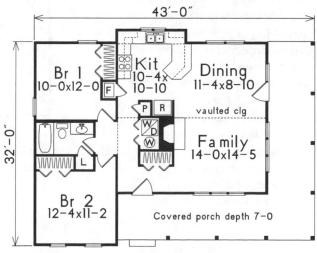

plan #588-008D-0149

price code AA

plan information

total living area:	1,160
bedrooms:	1
baths:	1
foundation type:	
crawl space	

special features

- kitchen/dining area combines with the laundry area creating a functional and organized space

- spacious vaulted living area has a large fireplace and is brightened by glass doors accessing the large deck

- ascend to the second floor loft by spiral stairs and find a cozy hideaway

- master bedroom is brightened by many windows and includes a private bath and double closets

second floor
200 sq. ft.

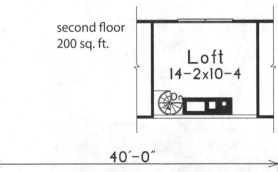

Loft
14-2x10-4

Dn

40'-0"

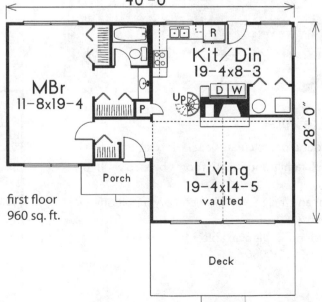

MBr
11-8x19-4

Kit/Din
19-4x8-3

Up

P

Living
19-4x14-5
vaulted

28'-0"

Porch

first floor
960 sq. ft.

Deck

plan #588-037D-0008

price code C

plan information

total living area:	1,707
bedrooms:	3
baths:	2
garage:	2-car
foundation type:	
slab	

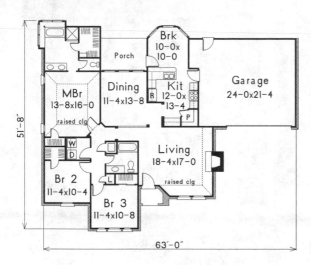

special features

- the formal living room off the entry hall has a high sloping ceiling and prominent fireplace
- kitchen and breakfast area allow access to an oversized garage and rear porch
- master bedroom has an impressive vaulted ceiling, luxurious bath, large walk-in closet and separate tub and shower
- utility room is conveniently located near the bedrooms

---

plan #588-060D-0018

price code A

plan information

total living area:	1,398
bedrooms:	3
baths:	2
garage:	2-car
foundation types:	
slab	
crawl space	
please specify when ordering	

special features

- country kitchen has a vaulted ceiling, spacious eating bar and lots of extra space for dining
- enormous vaulted great room has a cozy fireplace flanked by windows and ceiling beams for an added rustic appeal
- master suite bath has a shower and step-up tub with stained glass ledge and plant niche accents

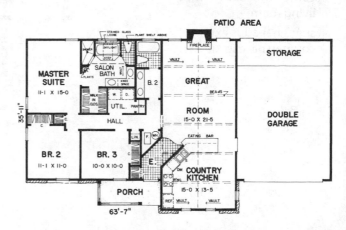

plan information

total living area:	1,484
bedrooms:	3
baths:	2
foundation type:	
basement	

special features

- energy efficient home with 2" x 6" exterior walls
- useful screened porch is ideal for dining and relaxing
- corner fireplace warms the living room
- snack bar adds extra counterspace in kitchen

first floor
908 sq. ft.

second floor
576 sq. ft.

plan #588-022D-0023

price code AA

plan information

total living area:	950
bedrooms:	2
baths:	1
garage:	1-car
foundation type:	
basement	

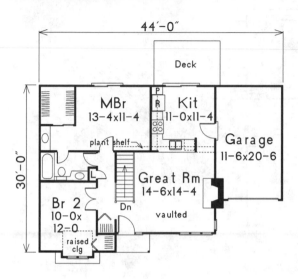

special features

- deck is attached to the kitchen, perfect for outdoor dining
- vaulted ceiling, open stairway and fireplace complement the great room
- bedroom #2 with a sloped ceiling and box-bay window can convert to a den
- master bedroom has a walk-in closet, plant shelf, separate dressing area and private access to bath
- kitchen has garage access and opens to the great room

---

plan #588-008D-0141

price code A

plan information

total living area:	1,211
bedrooms:	2
baths:	1
foundation types:	
crawl space standard	
basement	

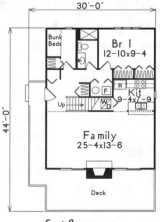

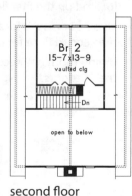

special features

- extraordinary views are enjoyed in the vaulted family room through sliding doors
- functional kitchen features snack bar and laundry closet
- bedroom and bunk room complete first floor while a large bedroom with two storage areas and balcony complete the second floor
- additional plan for second floor creates 223 square feet of additional bedroom space

first floor
884 sq. ft.

second floor
327 sq. ft.

plan #588-045D-0012

price code AA

plan information

total living area:	976
bedrooms:	3
baths:	1 1/2
foundation type:	
basement	

special features

- cozy front porch opens into the large living room
- convenient half bath is located on the first floor
- all bedrooms are located on the second floor for privacy
- dining room has access to the outdoors

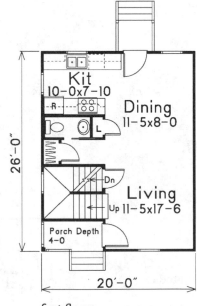

Kit
10-0x7-10

Dining
11-5x8-0

Living
Up 11-5x17-6

Dn

26'-0"

20'-0"

Porch Depth
4-0

first floor
488 sq. ft.

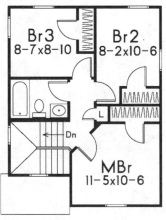

Br3
8-7x8-10

Br2
8-2x10-6

L

Dn

MBr
11-5x10-6

second floor
488 sq. ft.

plan #588-045D-0016

price code AA

plan information

total living area:	1,107
bedrooms:	3
baths:	2
foundation type:	
basement	

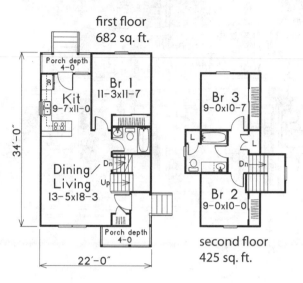

first floor
682 sq. ft.

second floor
425 sq. ft.

special features

- the L-shaped kitchen has a serving bar overlooking the dining/living room
- second floor bedrooms share a bath with linen closet
- front porch opens into foyer with convenient coat closet

---

plan #588-014D-0016

price code A

plan information

total living area:	1,426
bedrooms:	1
baths:	1
foundation type:	
crawl space	

special features

- energy efficient home with 2" x 6" exterior walls
- large front deck invites outdoor relaxation
- expansive windows, skylights, vaulted ceiling and fireplace enhance the living and dining room combination
- nook, adjacent to the living room, has a cozy window seat
- kitchen is open to the living and dining rooms

second floor
484 sq. ft.

first floor
942 sq. ft.

© Copyright Select Home Designs. All rights reserved.

plan information

total living area:	1,670
bedrooms:	3
baths:	2
foundation type: crawl space	

special features

- energy efficient home with 2" x 6" exterior walls
- living and dining areas combine making an ideal space for entertaining
- master bedroom accesses rear verandah through sliding glass doors
- second floor includes cozy family room with patio deck just outside of the secondary bedrooms

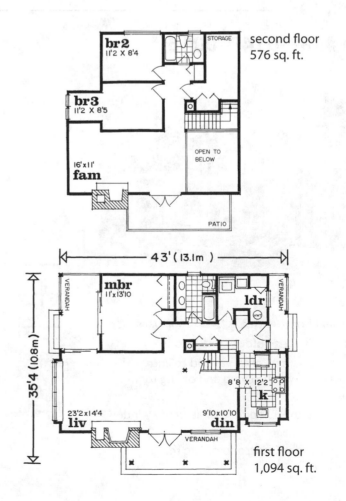

second floor
576 sq. ft.

first floor
1,094 sq. ft.

plan #588-022D-0017

price code A

plan information

total living area:	1,448
bedrooms:	3
baths:	2 1/2
garage:	2-car
foundation type:	
basement	

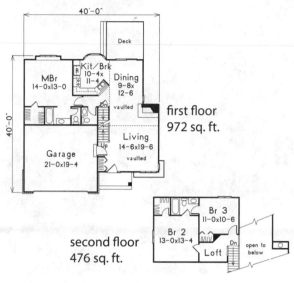

first floor
972 sq. ft.

second floor
476 sq. ft.

special features

- dining room conveniently adjoins kitchen and accesses rear deck
- private first floor master bedroom
- secondary bedrooms share a bath and cozy loft area

---

plan #588-084D-0032

price code D

special features

- the foyer conveniently houses a coat closet to help keep everything tidy
- the spacious owner's bedroom is a relaxing retreat and enjoys a private bath and two closets
- the U-shaped kitchen includes an abundance of counterspace and an island connecting it to the dining and great rooms

plan information

total living area:	1,543
bedrooms:	3
baths:	2
garage:	2-car carport
foundation types:	
basement	
crawl space	
slab	
please specify when ordering	

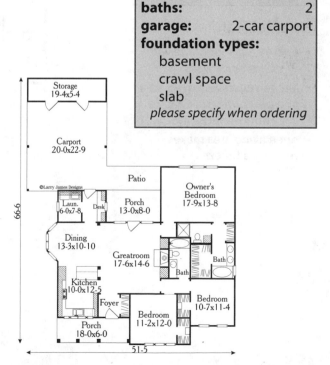

plan information

total living area:	1,442
bedrooms:	3
baths:	2
foundation type:	
basement	

special features

- energy efficient home with 2" x 6" exterior walls
- kitchen accesses bayed area and porch which provide a cozy atmosphere
- open living area makes relaxing a breeze

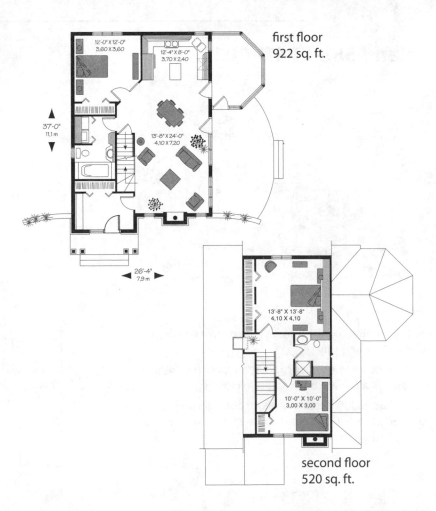

first floor
922 sq. ft.

second floor
520 sq. ft.

plan #588-037D-0022

price code B

plan information

total living area:	1,539
bedrooms:	3
baths:	2
garage:	2-car
foundation type:	
slab	

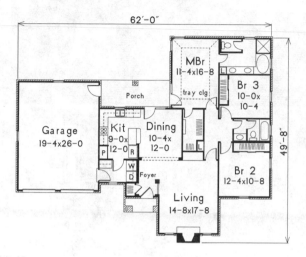

special features

- standard 9' ceilings
- master bedroom features 10' tray ceiling, access to porch, ample closet space and full bath
- serving counter separates kitchen and dining room
- foyer with handy coat closet opens to living area with fireplace
- handy utility room near kitchen

---

plan #588-040D-0013

price code A

plan information

total living area:	1,304
bedrooms:	3
baths:	2
garage:	2-car
foundation type:	
slab	

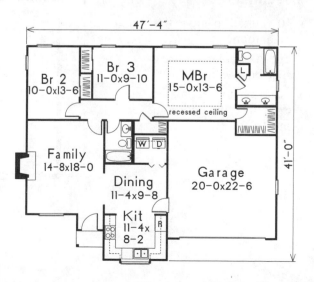

special features

- covered entrance leads into the family room with a cozy fireplace
- 10' ceilings in kitchen, dining and family rooms
- master bedroom features a coffered ceiling, walk-in closet and private bath
- efficient kitchen includes large window over the sink

plan #588-069D-0005

price code A

plan information

total living area:	1,267
bedrooms:	3
baths:	2
garage:	2-car

foundation types:
- slab
- crawl space

please specify when ordering

special features

- 10' vaulted ceiling in the great room
- open floor plan creates a spacious feeling
- master suite is separated from the other bedrooms for privacy

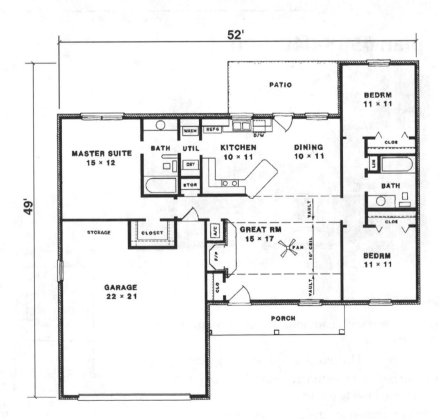

plan #588-048D-0001

price code D

plan information

total living area:	1,865
bedrooms:	4
baths:	2
garage:	2-car
foundation types:	
slab standard	
crawl space	

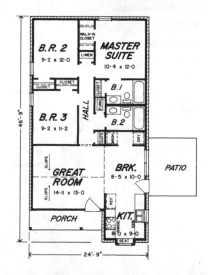

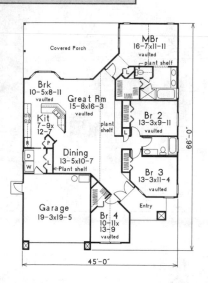

special features

- the large foyer opens into an expansive dining area and great room
- home features vaulted ceilings throughout
- master bedroom features an angled entry, vaulted ceiling, plant shelf and bath with double vanity, tub and shower

---

plan #588-060D-0013

price code AA

plan information

total living area:	1,053
bedrooms:	3
baths:	2
foundation types:	
slab	
crawl space	
please specify when ordering	

special features

- handy utility closet off the breakfast room
- sloped ceiling in great room adds a dramatic touch
- organized kitchen has everything close by for easy preparation

rear view

plan information

total living area:	1,470
bedrooms:	3
baths:	2

foundation types:
  basement
  crawl space
  slab
  please specify when ordering

special features

- vaulted breakfast room is cheerful and sunny
- private second floor master bedroom has a bath and walk-in closet
- large utility room has access to the outdoors

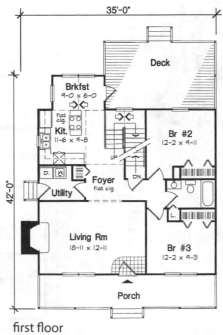

35'-0"

42'-0"

Deck

Brkfst
9-0 x 6-0

Flat clg.

Kit.
11-6 x 9-8

D.

Br #2
12-2 x 9-11

UP

Foyer
Flat clg.

Utility

DN

Living Rm
18-11 x 12-11

Br #3
12-2 x 9-3

Porch

first floor
1,035 sq. ft.

open to below

DN

Master Br
14-3 x 12-11

second floor
435 sq. ft.

plan #588-049D-0007

price code AA

plan information

total living area:	1,118
bedrooms:	2
baths:	2
garage:	2-car
foundation type:	
slab	

special features

- energy efficient home with 2" x 6" exterior walls
- convenient kitchen has direct access into garage and looks out onto front covered porch
- the covered patio is enjoyed by both the living room and master suite
- octagon-shaped dining room adds interest to the front exterior while the interior is sunny and bright

---

plan #588-058D-0010

price code AAA

plan information

total living area:	676
bedrooms:	1
baths:	1
foundation type:	
crawl space	

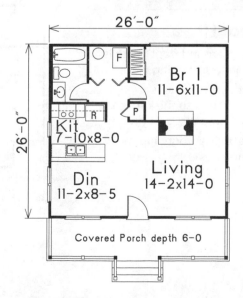

special features

- see-through fireplace between bedroom and living area adds character
- combined dining and living areas create an open feeling
- full-length front covered porch is perfect for enjoying the outdoors
- additional storage is available in the utility room
- 2" x 6" exterior walls available, please order plan #588-058D-0074

plan #588-039D-0007

price code B

plan information

total living area:	1,550
bedrooms:	3
baths:	2
garage:	2-car detached side entry

foundation types:
   slab
   crawl space
   please specify when ordering

special features

- wrap-around front porch is an ideal gathering place
- handy snack bar is positioned so the kitchen flows into the family room
- master bedroom has many amenities

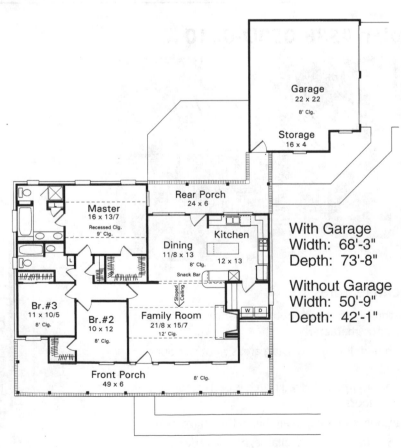

Garage
22 x 22
8' Clg.

Storage
16 x 4

Rear Porch
24 x 6

Master
16 x 13/7
Recessed Clg.
9' Clg.

Kitchen

Dining
11/8 x 13
8' Clg.

12 x 13

Snack Bar

Br. #3
11 x 10/5
8' Clg.

Br. #2
10 x 12
8' Clg.

Family Room
21/8 x 15/7
12' Clg.

Sloped Ceiling

W D

Front Porch
49 x 6

8' Clg.

With Garage
Width: 68'-3"
Depth: 73'-8"

Without Garage
Width: 50'-9"
Depth: 42'-1"

plan #588-058D-0014

price code AAA

plan information

total living area:	416
bedrooms:	sleeping area
baths:	1
foundation type:	
slab	

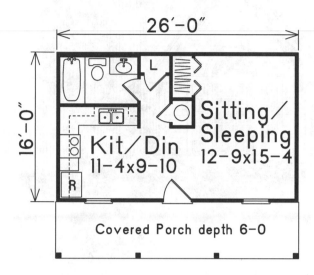

special features

- open floor plan creates a spacious feeling
- covered porch has rustic appeal
- the kitchen offers plenty of cabinets and workspace
- large linen closet is centrally located and close to the bath
- 2" x 6" exterior walls available, please order plan #588-058D-0076

---

plan #588-058D-0033

price code A

plan information

total living area:	1,440
bedrooms:	2
baths:	2
garage:	2-car side entry
foundation type:	
basement	

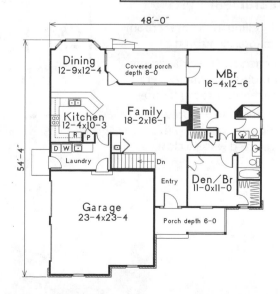

special features

- open floor plan with access to covered porches in front and back
- lots of linen, pantry and closet space throughout
- laundry/mud room between kitchen and garage is a convenient feature

plan #588-060D-0014

price code AA

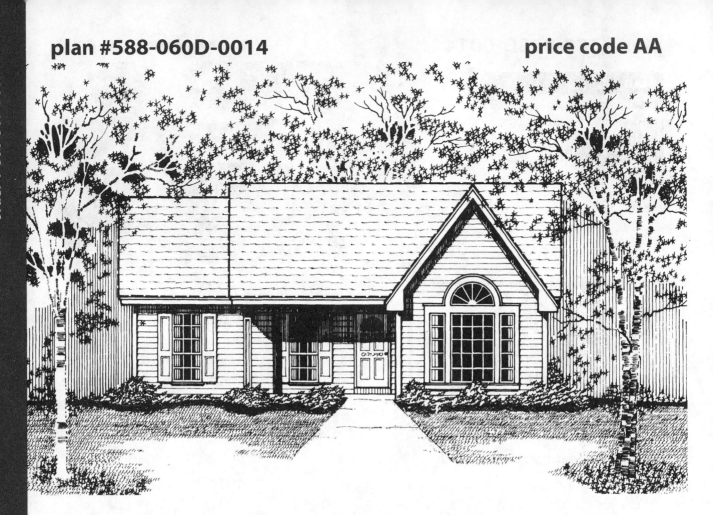

plan information

total living area:	1,021
bedrooms:	3
baths:	2
garage:	optional 2-car

foundation types:
slab
crawl space
please specify when ordering

special features

- 11' ceiling in the great room expands living area
- kitchen and breakfast room combine allowing easier preparation and cleanup
- master suite features a private bath and an oversized walk-in closet

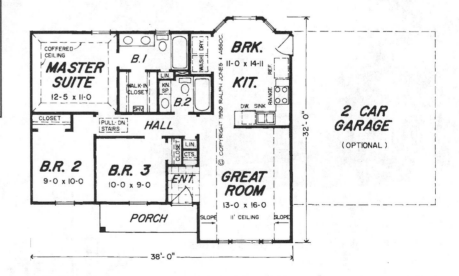

plan #588-040D-0029

order 1-800-367-7667

price code AA

plan information

total living area:	1,028
bedrooms:	3
baths:	1
foundation type:	
crawl space	

second floor
300 sq. ft.

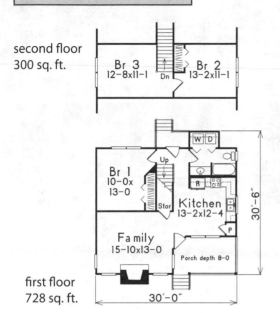

first floor
728 sq. ft.

special features

- well-designed bath contains laundry facilities
- the L-shaped kitchen has a handy pantry
- tall windows flank family room fireplace
- cozy covered porch provides unique angled entry into home

---

plan #588-045D-0017

price code AA

special features

- kitchen has a cozy bayed eating area
- master bedroom has a walk-in closet and private bath
- large great room has access to the back porch
- convenient coat closet is near the front entry

plan information

total living area:	954
bedrooms:	3
baths:	2
foundation type:	
basement	

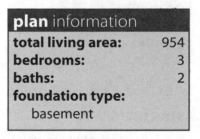

second floor
336 sq. ft.

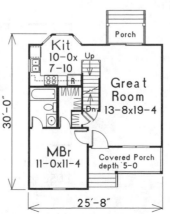

first floor
618 sq. ft.

plan #588-014D-0014

price code D

plan information

total living area:	1,921
bedrooms:	3
baths:	2 1/2
garage:	2-car
foundation type:	
basement	

special features

- energy efficient home with 2" x 6" exterior walls
- sunken family room includes a built-in entertainment center and coffered ceiling
- sunken formal living room features a coffered ceiling
- master bedroom dressing area has double sinks, spa tub, shower and French door to private deck
- large front porch adds to home's appeal

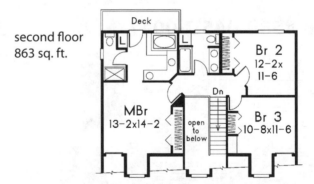

second floor
863 sq. ft.

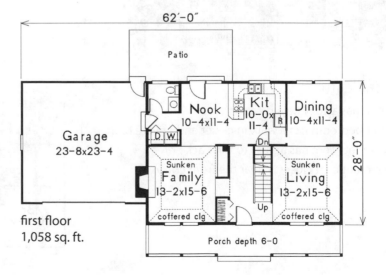

first floor
1,058 sq. ft.

plan #588-062D-0049

price code A

plan information

total living area:	1,292
bedrooms:	3
baths:	2
foundation type:	
crawl space	

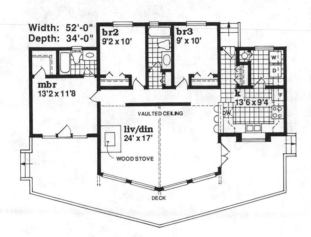

Width: 52'-0"
Depth: 34'-0"

special features

- energy efficient home with 2" x 6" exterior walls
- master bedroom features a walk-in closet, private bath and access to the outdoors onto an expansive deck
- prominent woodstove enhances the vaulted living/ dining area
- two secondary bedrooms share a bath
- kitchen has a convenient snack counter

---

plan #588-047D-0005

price code C

plan information

total living area:	1,885
bedrooms:	3
baths:	2
garage:	2-car side entry
foundation type:	
basement	

special features

- enormous covered patio
- dining and great rooms combine to create one large and versatile living area
- utility room is directly off the kitchen for convenience
- bonus room above garage has an additional 327 square feet of living space

Width: 52'-0"
Depth: 61'-6"

plan #588-055D-0067

price code A

plan information

total living area:	1,472
bedrooms:	4
baths:	2
foundation types:	
crawl space	
slab	
please specify when ordering	

special features

- 8' wrap-around porch entry is inviting and creates an outdoor living area
- great room has a rock hearth fireplace and is open to the second floor above
- side grilling porch has a cleaning sink for fish or game
- optional bonus room on the second floor has an additional 199 square feet of living area

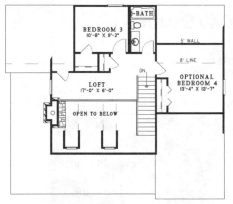

second floor
332 sq. ft.

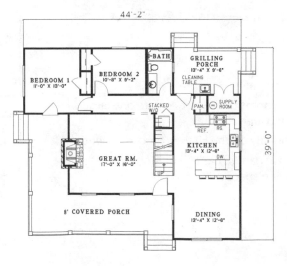

first floor
1,140 sq. ft.

plan #588-008D-0142

price code A

plan information

total living area:	1,224
bedrooms:	3
baths:	1
foundation type: crawl space	

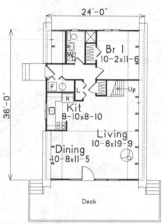

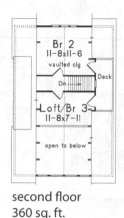

first floor
864 sq. ft.

second floor
360 sq. ft.

special features

- get away to this cozy A-frame featuring three bedrooms
- living and dining rooms with free-standing fireplace walk out onto a large deck
- the U-shaped kitchen has a unique built-in table at the end of the counter for intimate gatherings
- both second floor bedrooms enjoy their own private balcony

---

plan #588-022D-0021

price code AA

plan information

total living area:	1,020
bedrooms:	2
baths:	1
garage:	2-car
foundation type: basement	

special features

- kitchen features open stairs, pass-through to great room, pantry and deck access
- master bedroom features private entrance to bath, large walk-in closet and sliding doors to deck
- informal entrance into home through the garage
- great room has a vaulted ceiling and fireplace

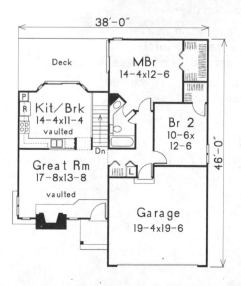

order 1-800-367-7667

plan information

total living area:	1,260
bedrooms:	3
baths:	1
foundation type:	
crawl space	

special features

- living area features an enormous stone fireplace and sliding glass doors for accessing the deck
- kitchen/dining area is organized with lots of cabinet and counterspace
- second bedroom is vaulted and has closet space along one entire wall

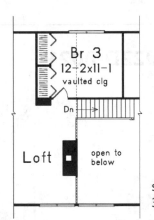

Br 3
12-2x11-1
vaulted clg

Dn

Loft
open to below

second floor
360 sq. ft.

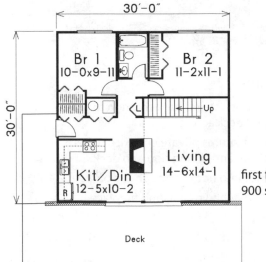

30'-0"

30'-0"

Br 1
10-0x9-11

Br 2
11-2x11-1

Up

Kit/Din
12-5x10-2

Living
14-6x14-1

R

first floor
900 sq. ft.

Deck

plan #588-039D-0004

price code A

plan information

total living area:	1,406
bedrooms:	3
baths:	2
garage:	2-car detached
foundation types:	
slab	
crawl space	
please specify when ordering	

With Garage
Width: 76'-6"
Depth: 57'-1"

Without Garage
Width: 47'-0"
Depth: 46'-0"

special features

- master bedroom has a sloped ceiling
- kitchen and dining area merge becoming a gathering place
- enter the family room from the charming covered front porch to find a fireplace and lots of windows

---

plan #588-013D-0005

price code A

plan information

total living area:	1,496
bedrooms:	3
baths:	2
garage:	2-car drive under
foundation type:	
basement	

special features

- vaulted living and dining rooms create a spacious feel to the main living areas
- breakfast area and kitchen combine for convenience
- large master bath has all the amenities
- dining area has access onto the deck

plan information

total living area:	991
bedrooms:	2
baths:	2
foundation type:	
basement	

special features

- energy efficient home with 2" x 6" exterior walls
- master bedroom has a large walk-in closet
- large and open kitchen is well organized

second floor
395 sq. ft.

11'-0" X 10'-4"
3,30 X 3,10

11'-8" X 11'-8"
3,50 X 3,50

first floor
596 sq. ft.

9'-4" X 10'-4"
2,80 X 3,10

26'-8"
8,0 m

8'-0" X 14'-4"
2,40 X 4,30

13'-0" X 12'-0"
3,90 X 3,60

10'-0" X 24'-0"
3,00 X 7,20

22'-8"
6,8 m

plan #588-007D-0081

price code A

plan information

total living area:	1,278
bedrooms:	3
baths:	1
garage:	2-car
foundation type:	
walk-out basement	

special features

- excellent U-shaped kitchen with garden window opens to an enormous great room with vaulted ceiling, fireplace and two skylights

- vaulted master bedroom offers a double-door entry, access to a deck and bath and two walk-in closets

- the bath has a double-bowl vanity and dramatic step-up garden tub with a lean-to greenhouse window

- 805 square feet of optional living area on the lower level with family room, bedroom #4 and bath

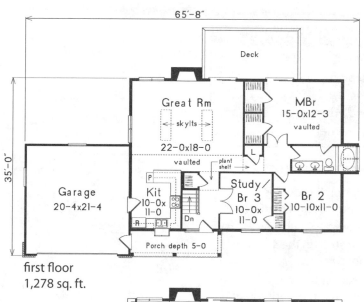

first floor
1,278 sq. ft.

optional
lower level

plan #588-045D-0013

price code AA

plan information

total living area:	1,085
bedrooms:	3
baths:	2
foundation type:	
basement	

special features

- rear porch provides handy access through the kitchen
- convenient hall linen closet is located on the second floor
- breakfast bar in the kitchen offers additional counterspace
- living and dining rooms combine for open living

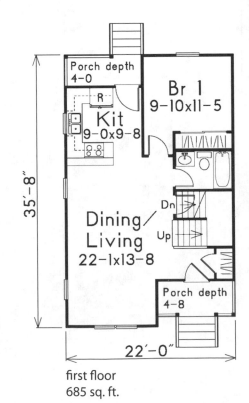

Porch depth 4-0

R

Kit
9-0x9-8

Br 1
9-10x11-5

35'-8"

Dining/
Living
22-1x13-8

Dn

Up

Porch depth 4-8

22'-0"

first floor
685 sq. ft.

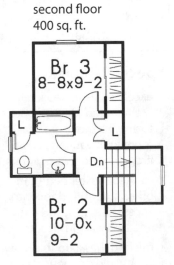

second floor
400 sq. ft.

Br 3
8-8x9-2

L

L

Dn

Br 2
10-0x
9-2

plan #588-022D-0003

plan information

total living area:	1,351
bedrooms:	2
baths:	2 1/2
garage:	2-car
foundation type:	
basement	

special features

- roof lines and vaulted ceilings make this home appear larger
- central fireplace provides a focal point for the dining and living areas
- master bedroom features a roomy window seat and a walk-in closet
- loft can easily be converted to a third bedroom

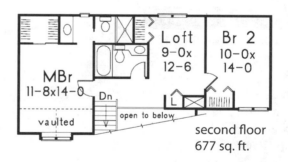

Loft
9-0x
12-6

Br 2
10-0x
14-0

MBr
11-8x14-0

Dn

vaulted

open to below

L

second floor
677 sq. ft.

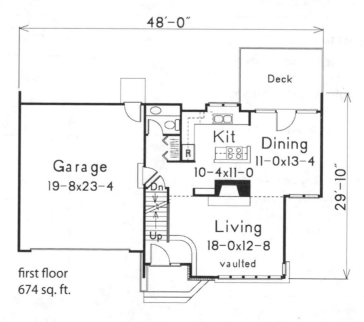

48′-0″

Deck

Garage
19-8x23-4

Kit
10-4x11-0

Dining
11-0x13-4

R

Dn

Up

Living
18-0x12-8
vaulted

29′-10″

first floor
674 sq. ft.

plan #588-076D-0017

price code B

plan information

total living area:	1,123
bedrooms:	3
baths:	2
garage:	1-car
foundation types:	
crawl space	
slab	
please specify when ordering	

special features

- spacious kitchen and breakfast area feature vaulted ceilings and patio access
- fireplace warms the adjoining family and dining rooms
- secondary bedrooms are secluded and share a bath

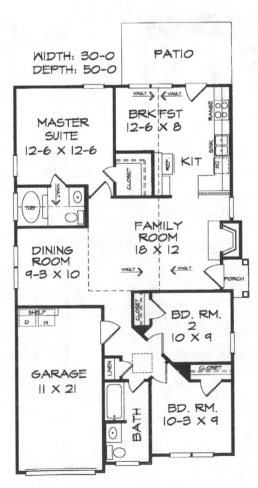

WIDTH: 30-0
DEPTH: 50-0

PATIO

MASTER SUITE 12-6 X 12-6

BRK'FST 12-6 X 8

RANGE

KIT

SINK

REF

TUB

WALK

CLOSET

FAMILY ROOM 18 X 12

VAULT

VAULT

PORCH

DINING ROOM 9-3 X 10

VAULT

VAULT

SHELF

D   W

CLOSET

BD. RM. 2 10 X 9

GARAGE 11 X 21

LINEN

CLOSET

BATH

BD. RM. 10-3 X 9

plan #588-040D-0030

price code B

plan information

total living area:	1,543
bedrooms:	3
baths:	2 1/2
garage:	2-car detached side entry
foundation types:	
slab standard	
crawl space	

special features

- fireplace serves as the focal point of the large family room
- efficient floor plan keeps hallways at a minimum
- laundry room connects the kitchen to the garage
- private first floor master bedroom has a walk-in closet and bath

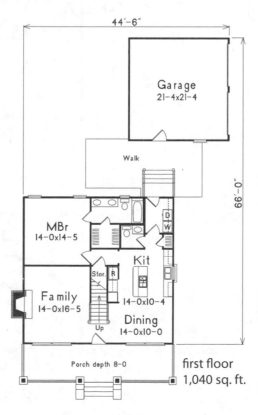

44'-6"

Garage
21-4x21-4

Walk

66'-0"

MBr
14-0x14-5

Kit
14-0x10-4

Stor. R

Family
14-0x16-5

Dining
14-0x10-0

Up

Porch depth 8-0

first floor
1,040 sq. ft.

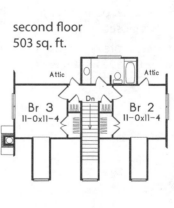

second floor
503 sq. ft.

Attic   Attic

Br 3
11-0x11-4

Dn

Br 2
11-0x11-4

plan #588-032D-0015

price code B

plan information

total living area:	1,556
bedrooms:	3
baths:	2
foundation type:	
basement	

special features

- energy efficient home with 2" x 6" exterior walls
- master bedroom has a walk-in closet
- separate entry with closet is a unique feature

second floor
604 sq. ft.

first floor
952 sq. ft.

plan #588-062D-0031

plan information

total living area:	1,073
bedrooms:	3
baths:	1 1/2

foundation types:
  basement
  crawl space
  please specify when ordering

special features

- the front-facing deck and covered balcony add to the outdoor living areas
- the fireplace is the main focus in the living room and effectively separates the living room from the dining room
- three large storage areas are found on the second floor

Width: 24'-0"
Depth: 36'-0"

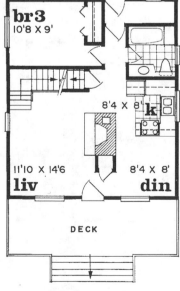

first floor
672 sq. ft.

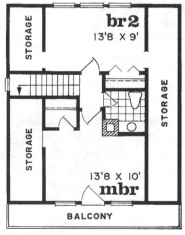

second floor
401 sq. ft.

plan #588-080D-0008

price code B

plan information

total living area:	1,644
bedrooms:	2
baths:	2
foundation type:	
crawl space	

special features

- energy efficient home with 2" x 6" exterior walls

- a highly versatile great room with a wrap-around covered porch encourages relaxed entertaining and is perfectly suited for evolving family activities

- the large U-shaped kitchen with raised breakfast bar is open to the great room ensuring that everyone is included in the fun

- the second floor vaulted studio has a private covered balcony and easily transforms this space into a home office

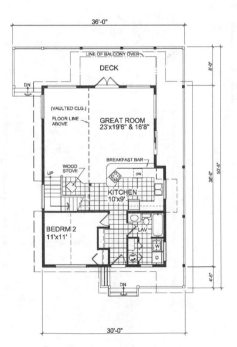

first floor
955 sq. ft.

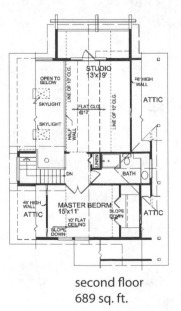

second floor
689 sq. ft.

plan #588-030D-0005   **price code C**

plan information

total living area:	1,815
bedrooms:	3
baths:	2
garage:	2-car side entry

foundation types:
- basement
- crawl space
- slab

please specify when ordering

special features

- well-designed kitchen opens to the dining room and features a raised breakfast bar
- first floor master suite has a walk-in closet
- front and back porches unite this home with the outdoors

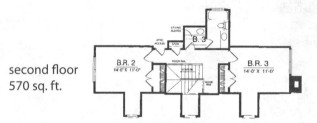

second floor
570 sq. ft.

Width: 47'-4"
Depth: 53'-6"

first floor
1,245 sq. ft.

order 1-800-367-7667

plan information

total living area:	1,565
bedrooms:	3
baths:	2 1/2
garage:	2-car
foundation type:	
basement	

special features

- highly-detailed exterior adds value
- large vaulted great room with a full wall of glass opens onto the corner deck
- loft balcony opens to rooms below and adds to the spacious feeling
- bay-windowed kitchen with a cozy morning room
- master bath features a platform tub, separate shower and a large walk-in closet

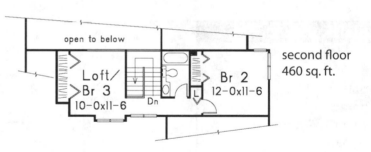

open to below

Loft/
Br 3
10-0x11-6

Dn

Br 2
12-0x11-6

second floor
460 sq. ft.

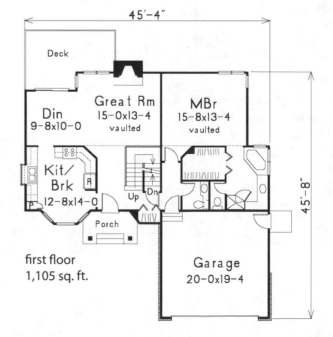

45'-4"

Deck

Din
9-8x10-0

Great Rm
15-0x13-4
vaulted

MBr
15-8x13-4
vaulted

Kit/
Brk
12-8x14-0

Up
Dn

45'-8"

Porch

first floor
1,105 sq. ft.

Garage
20-0x19-4

plan #588-084D-0026

order 1-800-367-7667

plan information

total living area:	1,551
bedrooms:	3
baths:	2
garage:	2-car
foundation types:	
basement	
crawl space	
slab	
please specify when ordering	

special features

- enter the home and view the spacious great room with grand fireplace flanked by built-ins
- the kitchen boasts a large island with seating and a built-in desk
- the private owner's bedroom enjoys a deluxe bath, porch access and nearby laundry closet
- the optional second floor has an additional 684 square feet of living area

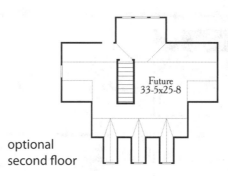

optional
second floor

Future
33-5x25-8

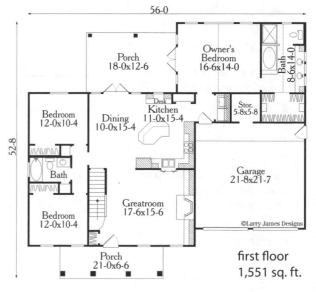

56-0

52-8

Porch
18-0x12-6

Owner's
Bedroom
16-6x14-0

Bath
8-6x14-0

Bedroom
12-0x10-4

Dining
10-0x15-4

Desk

Kitchen
11-0x15-4

Stor.
5-8x5-8

Bath

Garage
21-8x21-7

Bedroom
12-0x10-4

Greatroom
17-6x15-6

©Larry James Designs

Porch
21-0x6-6

first floor
1,551 sq. ft.

plan #588-062D-0051

price code B

plan information

total living area:	1,578
bedrooms:	3
baths:	2
garage:	2-car side entry

foundation types:
  basement
  crawl space
  please specify when ordering

special features

- energy efficient home with 2" x 6" exterior walls
- a fireplace warms the great room and is flanked by windows overlooking the rear deck
- bedrooms are clustered on one side of the home for privacy from living areas
- master bedroom has a unique art niche at its entry and a private bath with separate tub and shower

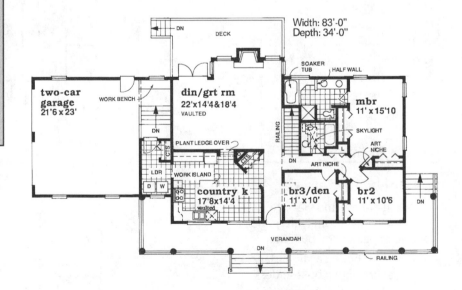

plan #588-008D-0160

plan information

total living area:	1,354
bedrooms:	2
baths:	1
foundation type:	
crawl space	

special features

- soaring ceilings highlight the kitchen, living and dining areas creating dramatic excitement
- a spectacular large deck surrounds the front and both sides of the home
- an impressive U-shaped kitchen has a wrap-around breakfast bar and shares fantastic views with the first and second floors through an awesome wall of glass
- two bedrooms with a bath, a sleeping loft and second floor balcony overlooking the living area complete the home

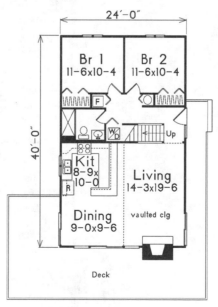

first floor
960 sq. ft.

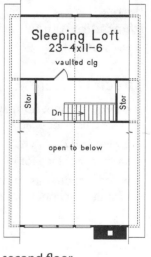

second floor
394 sq. ft.

plan #588-032D-0014

price code A

plan information

total living area:	1,258
bedrooms:	3
baths:	1 1/2
foundation type:	
basement	

special features

- energy efficient home with 2" x 6" exterior walls
- family and dining rooms share a fireplace for warmth
- powder room has laundry facilities for convenience

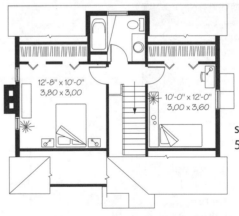

12'-8" X 10'-0"
3,80 x 3,00

10'-0" X 12'-0"
3,00 x 3,60

second floor
505 sq. ft.

12'-4" X 11'-4"
3,70 X 3,40

10'-8" X 8'-8"
3,20 X 2,60

25'-0"
7,5 m

15'-0" X 12'-4"
4,50 X 3,70

10'-0" X 9'-0"
3,00 X 2,70

first floor
753 sq. ft.

30'-0"
9,0 m

plan #588-052D-0032

plan information

total living area:	1,765
bedrooms:	3
baths:	2 1/2
garage:	2-car drive under
foundation type:	
basement	

special features

- a palladian window accenting the stone gable adds a new look to a popular cottage design
- dormers above open the vaulted living room
- kitchen extends to breakfast room with access to sundeck

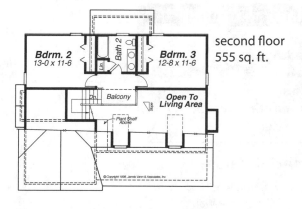

second floor
555 sq. ft.

Bdrm. 2
13-0 x 11-6

Bath 2

Bdrm. 3
12-8 x 11-6

Open To
Living Area

Balcony

Plant Shelf
Above

© Copyright 1996, Jannis Vann & Associates, Inc.

Sundeck
15-4 x 12-0

Brkfst.
12-0 x 7-4

Kit.
12-0 x 8-0

Dining
12-0 x 11-10

Ref.

M.Bath

Living
21-4 x 13-6

Master
Bdrm.
15-4 x 13-6

Dormer

Plant Shelf
Above

Dormer

first floor
1,210 sq. ft.

43-4

37-0

order 1-800-367-7667

plan information

total living area:	1,103
bedrooms:	2
baths:	1
garage:	1-car
foundation type:	
basement	

special features

- energy efficient home with 2" x 6" exterior walls
- all bedrooms in one area of the house for privacy
- bay window enhances dining area
- living and dining areas combine for a spacious feeling

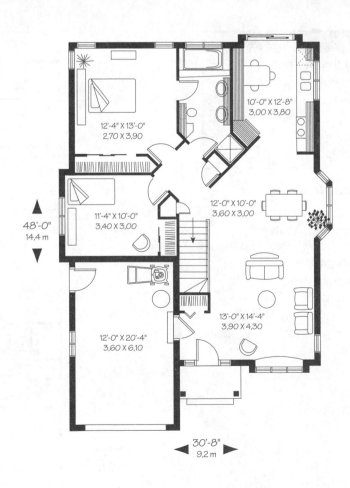

12'-4" X 13'-0"
2,70 X 3,90

10'-0" X 12'-8"
3,00 X 3,80

11'-4" X 10'-0"
3,40 X 3,00

12'-0" X 10'-0"
3,60 X 3,00

48'-0"
14,4 m

13'-0" X 14'-4"
3,90 X 4,30

12'-0" X 20'-4"
3,60 X 6,10

30'-8"
9,2 m

plan #588-032D-0038

price code AA

plan information

total living area:	1,056
bedrooms:	2
baths:	1 1/2
foundation type:	
basement	

special features

- energy efficient home with 2" x 6" exterior walls
- unique fireplace becomes focal point in living and dining areas
- three-season room off living area is cheerful and bright
- galley-style kitchen is efficiently designed

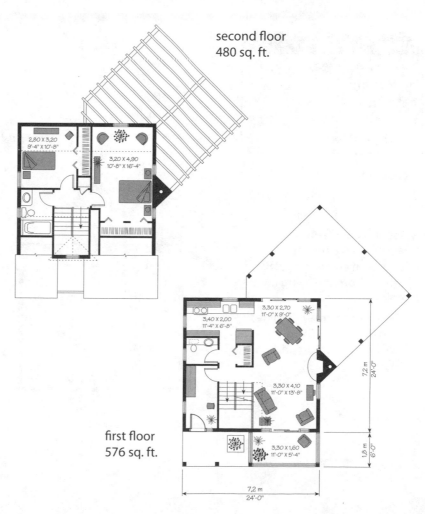

second floor
480 sq. ft.

first floor
576 sq. ft.

plan #588-032D-0035

price code A

plan information

total living area:	1,304
bedrooms:	2
baths:	1
foundation type:	
crawl space	

special features

- energy efficient home with 2" x 6" exterior walls
- second floor features a sitting area near the bedroom creating a relaxing retreat from the living area below
- large dining area combines with living area for maximum comfort and space

first floor
945 sq. ft.

second floor
359 sq. ft.

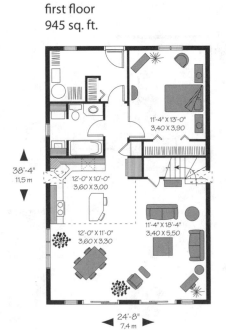

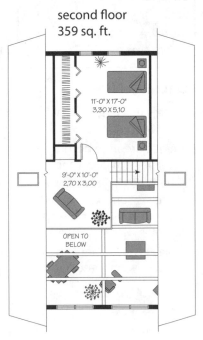

plan #588-008D-0076

plan information

total living area:	1,922
bedrooms:	3
baths:	2 1/2
foundation type:	
basement	

special features

- master bedroom includes many luxuries such as an oversized private bath and large walk-in closet
- the kitchen is spacious with a functional eat-in breakfast bar and is adjacent to the nook which is ideal as a breakfast room
- plenty of storage is featured in both bedrooms on the second floor and in the hall
- enormous utility room is centrally located on the first floor

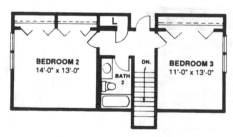

second floor
519 sq. ft.

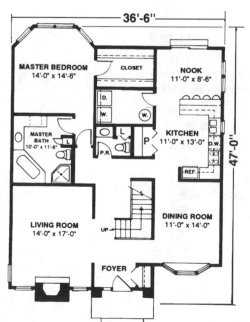

first floor
1,403 sq. ft.

plan #588-045D-0014

price code AA

plan information

total living area:	987
bedrooms:	3
baths:	1
foundation type:	
basement	

special features

- galley kitchen opens into the cozy breakfast room
- convenient coat closets are located by both entrances
- dining/living room offers an expansive open area
- breakfast room has access to the outdoors
- front porch is great for enjoying outdoor living

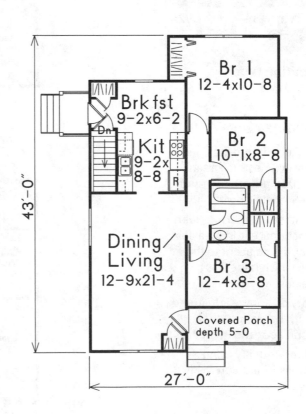

plan #588-022D-0004

plan information

total living area:	1,359
bedrooms:	3
baths:	2 1/2
garage:	2-car
foundation type:	
basement	

special features

- covered porch, stone chimney and abundant windows lend an outdoor appeal
- spacious and bright kitchen has pass-through to formal dining room
- large walk-in closets in all bedrooms
- extensive deck expands dining and entertaining areas

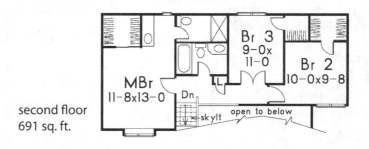

second floor
691 sq. ft.

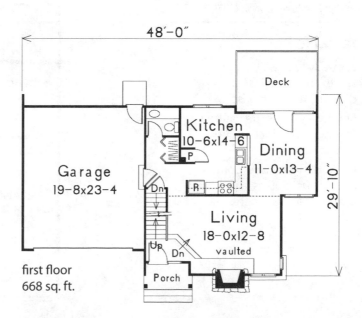

first floor
668 sq. ft.

plan information

total living area:	1,116
bedrooms:	3
baths:	2
garage:	1-car
foundation types:	
crawl space	
slab	
please specify when ordering	

special features

- centrally located kitchen serves the breakfast and dining areas with ease
- fireplace warms the vaulted family room which is open and spacious
- vaulted master bedroom enjoys two closets, a private bath and access to the outdoors

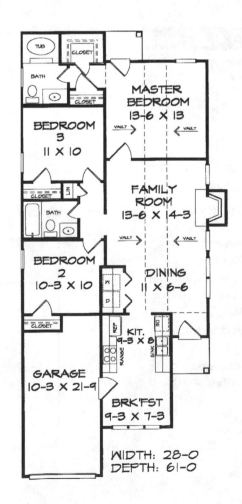

WIDTH: 28-0
DEPTH: 61-0

plan #588-049D-0004

price code C

plan information

total living area:	1,997
bedrooms:	3
baths:	2 1/2
foundation type:	
basement	

special features

- energy efficient home with 2" x 6" exterior walls
- screened porch leads to a rear terrace with access to the breakfast room
- living and dining rooms combine adding spaciousness to the floor plan
- other welcome amenities include boxed windows in the breakfast and dining rooms, a fireplace in the living room and a pass-through snack bar in the kitchen

rear view

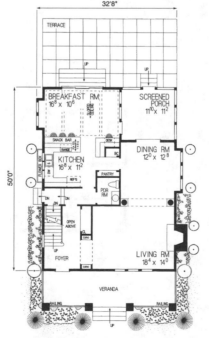

first floor
1,111 sq. ft.

second floor
886 sq. ft.

plan information

total living area:	796
bedrooms:	1
baths:	1
foundation type:	
crawl space	

special features

- energy efficient home with 2" x 6" exterior walls

- this home is perfect for a narrow lot

- the second floor sleeping loft has the ability to be partitioned for additional privacy

- the covered front entry is protected from the elements and adds to the curb appeal

first floor
560 sq. ft.

second floor
236 sq. ft.

plan #588-007D-0103

plan information

total living area:	1,231
bedrooms:	2
baths:	2
garage:	1-car drive under
foundation type:	
walk-out basement	

special features

- dutch gables and stone accents provide an enchanting appearance

- the spacious living room offers a masonry fireplace, atrium with window wall and is open to a dining area with bay window

- kitchen has a breakfast counter, lots of cabinet space and glass sliding doors to a balcony

- 380 square feet of optional living area on the lower level

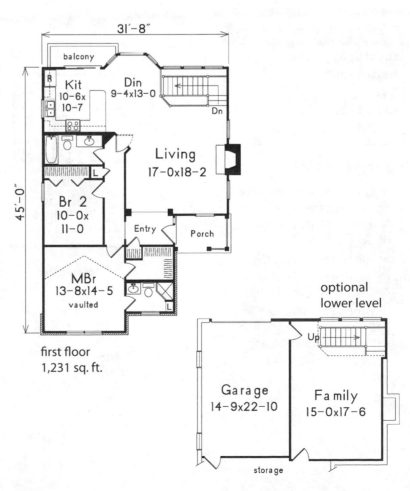

first floor
1,231 sq. ft.

optional lower level

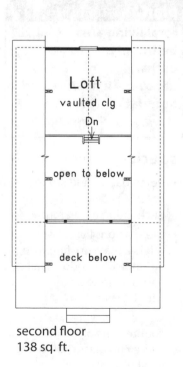

order 1-800-367-7667

plan information

total living area:	618
bedrooms:	1
baths:	1
foundation type:	
pier	

special features

- memorable family events are certain to be enjoyed on this fabulous partially covered deck

- equally impressive is the living area with its cathedral ceiling and exposed rafters

- a kitchenette, bedroom and bath conclude the first floor with a delightful sleeping loft on the second floor

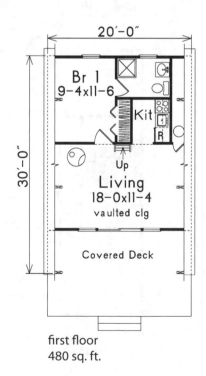

first floor
480 sq. ft.

second floor
138 sq. ft.

plan #588-001D-0043

plan information

total living area:	1,104
bedrooms:	3
baths:	2
foundation types:	

crawl space standard
basement
slab

special features

- master bedroom includes a private bath
- convenient side entrance to the dining area/kitchen
- laundry area is located near the kitchen
- large living area creates a comfortable atmosphere

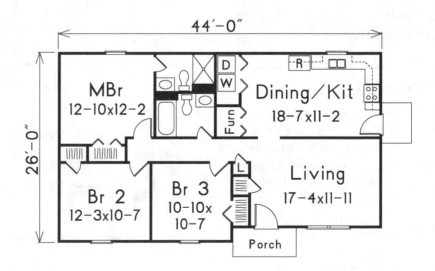

plan #588-058D-0011

price code AA

plan information

total living area:	924
bedrooms:	2
baths:	1
foundation type:	
slab	

special features

- box-bay window seats brighten the interior while enhancing the front facade
- spacious kitchen with lots of cabinet space and large pantry
- a T-shaped covered porch is screened for added enjoyment
- plenty of closet space throughout with linen closets in both bedrooms

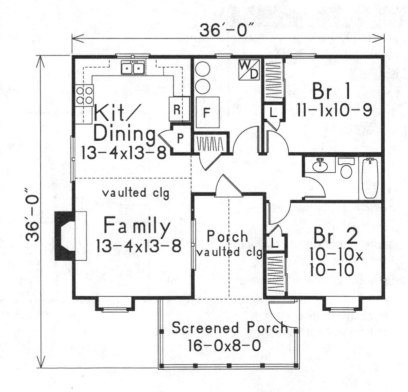

plan #588-022D-0006

plan information

total living area:	1,443
bedrooms:	3
baths:	2
garage:	2-car
foundation type:	
basement	

special features

- raised foyer and cathedral ceiling in living room
- impressive tall-wall fireplace between living and dining rooms
- open U-shaped kitchen features a cheerful breakfast bay
- angular side deck accentuates patio and garden
- first floor master bedroom has a walk-in closet and a corner window

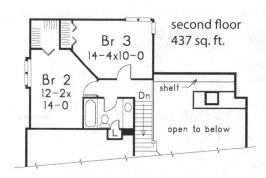

second floor
437 sq. ft.

Br 3
14-4x10-0

Br 2
12-2x
14-0

Dn

shelf

open to below

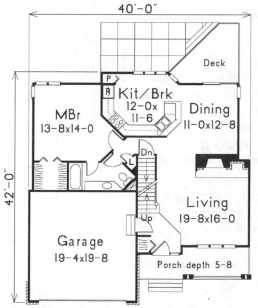

40'-0"

42'-0"

Deck

P
R

Kit/Brk
12-0x
11-6

MBr
13-8x14-0

Dining
11-0x12-8

Dn
L

Living
19-8x16-0

Up

Garage
19-4x19-8

Porch depth 5-8

first floor
1,006 sq. ft.

plan #588-084D-0008

price code D

plan information

total living area:	1,745
bedrooms:	3
baths:	2
garage:	2-car side entry
foundation types:	
basement	
crawl space	
slab	
please specify when ordering	

special features

- decorative columns separate the formal dining room from the great room while maintaining openness

- a symmetrically designed kitchen with two pantries offers full function

- two sets of French doors flank the handsome fireplace in the great room

- the future second floor has an additional 922 square feet of living area

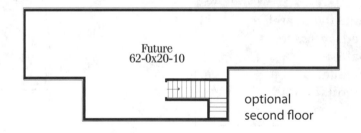

Future
62-0x20-10

optional
second floor

W: 63'- 0"
D: 41'- 0"

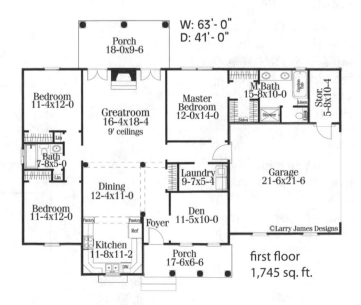

Porch
18-0x9-6

Bedroom
11-4x12-0

Greatroom
16-4x18-4
9' ceilings

Master
Bedroom
12-0x14-0

M. Bath
15-8x10-0

Stor.
5-8x10-4

Bath
7-8x5-0

Bedroom
11-4x12-0

Dining
12-4x11-0

Laundry
9-7x5-4

Den
11-5x10-0

Garage
21-6x21-6

Foyer

Pantry
Ref

Kitchen
11-8x11-2

Porch
17-6x6-6

©Larry James Designs

first floor
1,745 sq. ft.

plan #588-008D-0150

price code B

plan information

total living area:	1,680
bedrooms:	5
baths:	2 1/2
foundation type:	
basement	

special features

- highly functional lower level includes a wet hall with storage, laundry area, workshop and cozy ski lounge with an enormous fireplace
- first floor is warmed by a large fireplace in the living/dining area which features a spacious wrap-around deck
- lots of sleeping space for guests or a large family

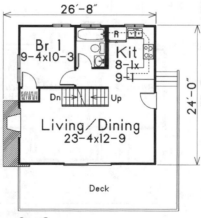

first floor
576 sq. ft.

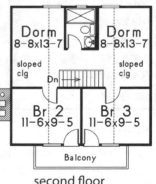

second floor
528 sq. ft.

lower level
576 sq. ft.

plan information

total living area:	1,735
bedrooms:	3
baths:	2 1/2
garage:	2-car drive under
foundation type:	basement

special features

- angled kitchen wall expands space into the dining room
- second floor has a cozy sitting area with cheerful window
- two spacious bedrooms on the second floor share a bath

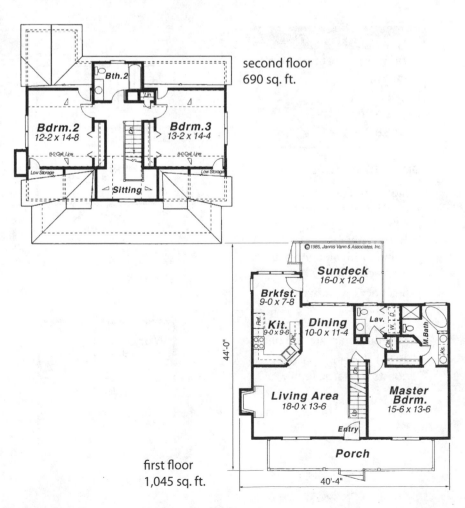

second floor
690 sq. ft.

first floor
1,045 sq. ft.

plan #588-049D-0009

plan information

total living area:	1,673
bedrooms:	3
baths:	2
foundation type:	
crawl space	

special features

- energy efficient home with 2" x 6" exterior walls
- great room flows into the breakfast nook with outdoor access and beyond to an efficient kitchen
- master bedroom on the second floor has access to a loft/study, private balcony and bath
- covered porch surrounds the entire home for outdoor living area

second floor
580 sq. ft.

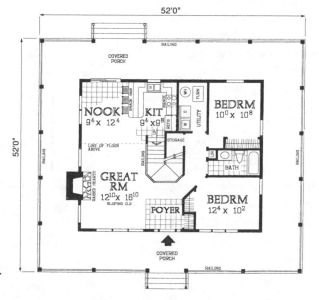

first floor
1,093 sq. ft.

plan information

total living area:	1,339
bedrooms:	3
baths:	2 1/2
foundation type:	
crawl space	

special features

- full-length covered porch enhances front facade
- vaulted ceiling and stone fireplace add drama to the family room
- walk-in closets in the bedrooms provide ample storage space
- combined kitchen/dining area adjoins the family room for the perfect entertaining space
- 2" x 6" exterior walls available, please order plan #588-058D-0072

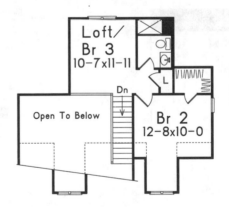

second floor
415 sq. ft.

Loft/Br 3
10-7x11-11

Open To Below

Dn

Br 2
12-8x10-0

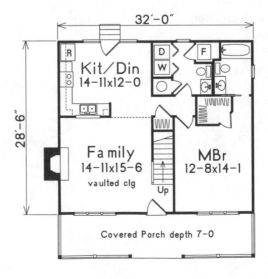

32'-0"

28'-6"

Kit/Din
14-11x12-0

Family
14-11x15-6
vaulted clg

Up

MBr
12-8x14-1

Covered Porch depth 7-0

first floor
924 sq. ft.

plan #588-001D-0072

price code A

plan information

total living area:	1,288
bedrooms:	3
baths:	2
foundation types:	
crawl space standard	
basement	
slab	

special features

- kitchen, dining area and great room join to create an open living space
- master bedroom includes a private bath
- secondary bedrooms enjoy ample closet space
- hall bath features a convenient laundry closet
- dining room accesses the outdoors

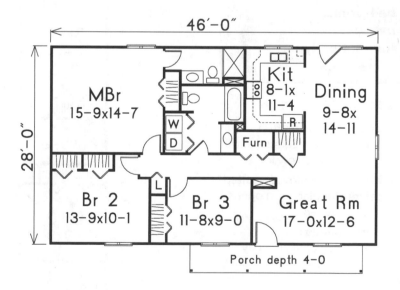

plan information

total living area:	1,161
bedrooms:	3
baths:	2
foundation type:	
basement	

special features

- brickwork and feature window add elegance to this home for a narrow lot
- living room enjoys a vaulted ceiling, fireplace and opens to the kitchen
- the U-shaped kitchen offers a breakfast area with bay window, snack bar and built-in pantry

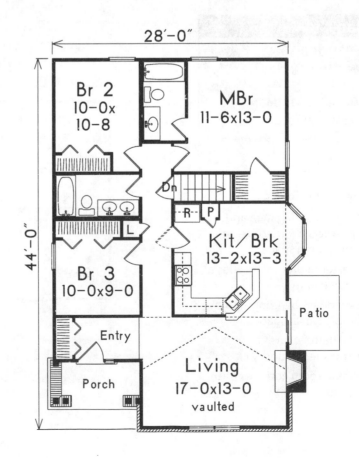

28'-0"

44'-0"

Br 2
10-0x 10-8

MBr
11-6x13-0

Dn

R P

Kit/Brk
13-2x13-3

Br 3
10-0x9-0

Entry

Patio

Porch

Living
17-0x13-0
vaulted

plan #588-008D-0139

price code A

plan information

total living area:	1,272
bedrooms:	3
baths:	1 1/2
foundation type:	
crawl space	

special features

- stone fireplace accents living room
- spacious kitchen includes snack bar overlooking the living room
- first floor bedroom is roomy and secluded
- plenty of closet space for second floor bedrooms plus a generous balcony which wraps around the second floor

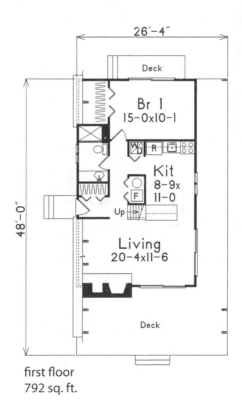

26'-4"

Deck

Br 1
15-0x10-1

Kit
8-9x
11-0

Up

Living
20-4x11-6

48'-0"

Deck

first floor
792 sq. ft.

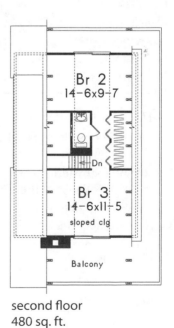

Br 2
14-6x9-7

Dn

Br 3
14-6x11-5
sloped clg

Balcony

second floor
480 sq. ft.

plan information

total living area:	1,189
bedrooms:	3
baths:	2 1/2
garage:	2-car
foundation type:	
basement	

special features

- all bedrooms are located on the second floor
- dining room and kitchen both have views of the patio
- convenient half bath is located near the kitchen
- master bedroom has a private bath

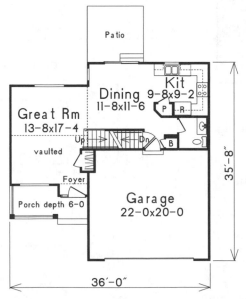

first floor
615 sq. ft.

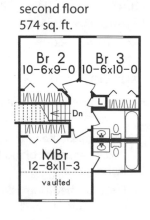

second floor
574 sq. ft.

plan #588-032D-0040

price code A

plan information

total living area:	1,480
bedrooms:	2
baths:	2
foundation type:	
basement	

special features

- energy efficient home with 2" x 6" exterior walls
- cathedral ceilings in the family and dining rooms
- master bedroom has a walk-in closet and access to bath

second floor
456 sq. ft.

first floor
1,024 sq. ft.

plan information

total living area:	1,191
bedrooms:	3
baths:	2
garage:	2-car side entry
foundation types:	
slab standard	
crawl space	

special features

- energy efficient home with 2" x 6" exterior walls
- master bedroom is located near living areas for maximum convenience
- living room has a cathedral ceiling and stone fireplace

plan #588-035D-0004

price code A

plan information

total living area:	1,425
bedrooms:	3
baths:	2
garage:	2-car
foundation types:	

   crawl space

   slab

   walk-out basement

please specify when ordering

special features

• kitchen and vaulted breakfast room are the center of activity

• a corner fireplace warms the spacious family room

• oversized serving bar extends seating in dining room

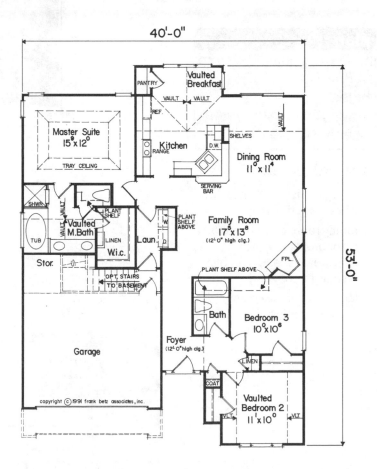

plan information

total living area:	1,468
bedrooms:	3
baths:	2
foundation type:	
basement	

special features

- energy efficient home with 2" x 6" exterior walls
- family room has a beautiful cathedral ceiling adding spaciousness and a fireplace creating a cozy feel
- large kitchen has plenty of room for dining

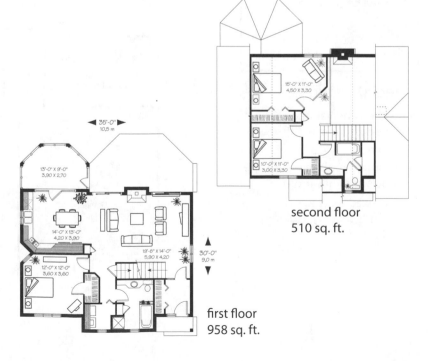

rear view

second floor
510 sq. ft.

first floor
958 sq. ft.

35'-0"
10,5 m

30'-0"
9,0 m

13'-0" X 9'-0"
3,90 x 2,70

14'-0" X 13'-0"
4,20 x 3,90

12'-0" X 12'-0"
3,60 x 3,60

19'-8" X 14'-0"
5,90 X 4,20

15'-0" X 11'-0"
4,50 X 3,30

10'-0" X 11'-0"
3,00 X 3,30

plan #588-001D-0067

order 1-800-367-7667

plan information

total living area:	1,285
bedrooms:	3
baths:	2

foundation types:
crawl space standard
basement
slab

special features

- accommodating home with ranch-style porch
- large storage area on back of home
- master bedroom includes dressing area, private bath and built-in bookcase
- kitchen features pantry, breakfast bar and complete view to the dining room

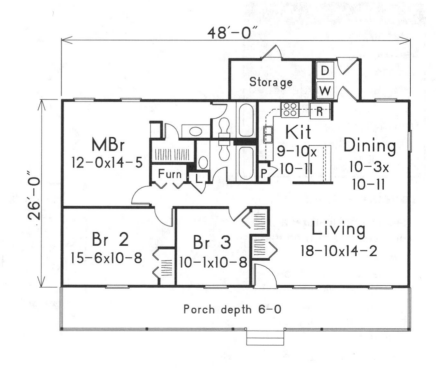

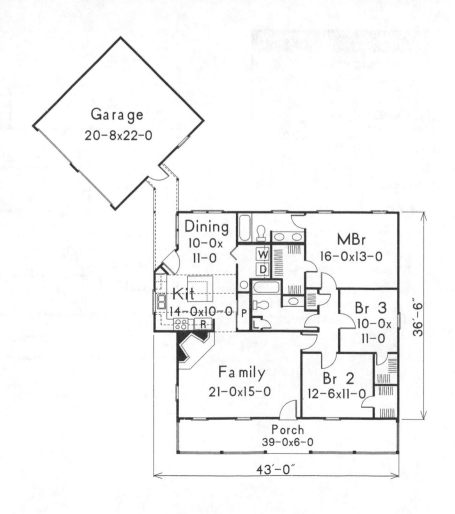

plan information

total living area:	1,475
bedrooms:	3
baths:	2
garage:	2-car detached side entry

foundation types:
  slab standard
  crawl space

special features

- family room features a high ceiling and prominent corner fireplace
- kitchen with island counter and garden window makes a convenient connection between the family and dining rooms
- hallway leads to three bedrooms all with large walk-in closets
- covered breezeway joins the main house and garage
- full-width covered porch entry lends a country touch

Garage
20-8x22-0

Dining
10-0x
11-0

MBr
16-0x13-0

Kit
14-0x10-0

Family
21-0x15-0

Br 3
10-0x
11-0

Br 2
12-6x11-0

Porch
39-0x6-0

36'-6"

43'-0"

our blueprint packages offer...

Quality plans for building your future, with extras that provide unsurpassed value, ensure good construction and long-term enjoyment.

A quality home - one that looks good, functions well, and provides years of enjoyment - is a product of many things - design, materials, craftsmanship.

But it's also the result of outstanding blueprints - the actual plans and specifications that tell the builder exactly how to build your home.

And with our BLUEPRINT PACKAGES you get the absolute best. A complete set of blueprints is available for every design in this book. These "working drawings" are highly detailed, resulting in two key benefits:

☐ Better understanding by the contractor of how to build your home and...

☐ More accurate construction estimates.

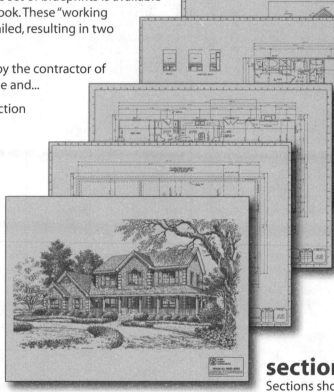

cover sheet

Included with many of our plans, the cover sheet is the artist's rendering of the exterior of the home. It will give you an idea of how your home will look when completed and landscaped.

interior elevations

Interior elevations provide views of special interior elements such as fireplaces, kitchen cabinets, built-in units and other features of the home.

foundation plan

The foundation plan shows the layout of the basement, crawl space, slab or pier foundation. All necessary notations and dimensions are included. See plan page for the foundation types included. If the home plan you choose does not have your desired foundation type, our Customer Service Representatives can advise you on how to customize your foundation to suit your specific needs or site conditions.

details

Details show how to construct certain components of your home, such as the roof system, stairs, deck, etc.

sections

Sections show detail views of the home or portions of the home as if it were sliced from the roof to the foundation. This sheet shows important areas such as load-bearing walls, stairs, joists, trusses and other structural elements, which are critical for proper construction.

floor plan

The floor plans show the placement of walls, doors, closets, plumbing fixtures, electrical outlets, columns, and beams for each level of the home.

exterior elevations

Exterior elevations illustrate the front, rear and both sides of the house, with all details of exterior materials and the required dimensions.

home plans index

plan number	square feet	price code	page	material list	right reading rev.	canada shipping
588-001D-0018	988	AA	73	•		
588-001D-0019	1,314	A	28	•		
588-001D-0021	1,416	A	65	•		
588-001D-0024	1,360	A	124	•		
588-001D-0031	1,501	B	137	•		
588-001D-0034	1,642	B	46	•		
588-001D-0035	1,396	A	69	•		
588-001D-0036	1,320	A	117	•		
588-001D-0040	864	AAA	9	•		
588-001D-0041	1,000	AA	144	•		
588-001D-0043	1,104	AA	235	•		
588-001D-0060	1,818	C	173	•		
588-001D-0061	1,875	C	60	•		
588-001D-0067	1,285	B	251	•		
588-001D-0072	1,288	A	243	•		
588-001D-0077	1,769	B	34	•		
588-001D-0081	1,160	AA	87	•		
588-001D-0085	720	AAA	57	•		
588-001D-0086	1,154	AA	140	•		
588-001D-0087	1,230	A	76	•		
588-001D-0088	800	AAA	49	•		
588-001D-0093	1,120	AA	147	•		
588-004D-0002	1,823	C	12	•		
588-007D-0028	1,711	B	15	•		
588-007D-0029	576	AAA	73	•		
588-007D-0030	1,140	AA	128	•		
588-007D-0031	1,092	AA	139	•		
588-007D-0032	1,294	A	177	•		
588-007D-0037	1,403	A	27	•		
588-007D-0038	1,524	B	126	•		
588-007D-0039	1,563	B	52	•		
588-007D-0042	914	AA	47	•		
588-007D-0043	647	AAA	64	•		
588-007D-0045	1,321	A	83	•		
588-007D-0060	1,268	B	11	•		
588-007D-0068	1,384	B	134	•		
588-007D-0075	1,684	B	115	•		
588-007D-0081	1,278	A	209	•		
588-007D-0102	1,452	A	8	•		
588-007D-0103	1,231	A	233	•		
588-007D-0104	969	AA	55	•		
588-007D-0105	1,084	AA	112	•		
588-007D-0106	1,200	A	37	•		
588-007D-0107	1,161	AA	244	•		
588-007D-0109	888	AAA	31	•		
588-007D-0110	1,169	AA	151	•		
588-008D-0072	1,200	A	75	•		
588-008D-0076	1,922	C	227	•		
588-008D-0132	1,209	A	65	•		
588-008D-0133	624	AAA	83	•		
588-008D-0134	1,275	A	129	•		
588-008D-0136	1,106	AA	101	•		
588-008D-0137	1,312	A	151	•		
588-008D-0138	1,280	A	169	•		
588-008D-0139	1,272	A	245	•		
588-008D-0140	1,391	A	29	•		
588-008D-0141	1,211	A	187	•		
588-008D-0142	1,224	A	205	•		
588-008D-0143	1,299	A	51	•		
588-008D-0144	1,176	AA	53	•		
588-008D-0145	1,750	B	179	•		
588-008D-0147	1,316	A	148	•		
588-008D-0148	784	AAA	166	•		
588-008D-0149	1,160	AA	184			
588-008D-0150	1,680	B	239	•		
588-008D-0152	1,260	A	206	•		
588-008D-0153	792	AAA	33	•		
588-008D-0154	527	AAA	35	•		
588-008D-0155	1,200	A	17	•		
588-008D-0158	1,584	B	91	•		
588-008D-0159	733	AAA	153	•		
588-008D-0160	1,354	A	221	•		
588-008D-0161	618	AAA	234	•		
588-008D-0162	865	AAA	161	•		
588-010D-0003	1,560	B	88	•		
588-010D-0006	1,170	AA	141	•		
588-013D-0001	1,050	AA	79			
588-013D-0005	1,496	A	207			
588-013D-0011	1,643	B	121			
588-014D-0005	1,314	A	79	•		
588-014D-0014	1,921	D	202	•		
588-014D-0016	1,426	A	189	•		
588-015D-0009	960	AA	171			
588-015D-0023	1,649	B	95		•	
588-015D-0037	2,202	D	162			
588-016D-0007	1,207	A	131	•		
588-016D-0009	1,416	A	63	•		
588-016D-0014	1,677	B	45	•		
588-016D-0030	1,303	A	103	•		
588-016D-0031	1,648	C	26	•		
588-016D-0032	1,496	A	19	•		
588-016D-0033	1,563	B	36	•		
588-016D-0041	1,097	B	85	•		
588-016D-0062	1,380	B	122	•		
588-016D-0066	1,029	AA	67	•		
588-017D-0005	1,367	B	81	•		
588-017D-0008	1,466	B	69	•		
588-017D-0009	1,432	B	87	•		
588-017D-0010	1,660	C	7	•		
588-020D-0001	1,375	A	105			
588-020D-0014	1,150	AA	155			
588-020D-0015	1,191	AA	248			
588-021D-0006	1,600	C	54	•		
588-021D-0008	1,266	A	174	•		
588-021D-0016	1,600	B	72	•		
588-022D-0001	1,039	AA	100	•		
588-022D-0002	1,246	A	90	•		
588-022D-0003	1,351	A	211	•		
588-022D-0004	1,359	A	229	•		
588-022D-0005	1,360	A	40	•		
588-022D-0006	1,443	A	237	•		
588-022D-0007	1,516	B	123	•		
588-022D-0008	1,565	B	218	•		
588-022D-0011	1,630	B	18	•		
588-022D-0012	1,550	B	61	•		
588-022D-0017	1,448	A	191	•		
588-022D-0018	1,368	A	142	•		
588-022D-0019	1,283	A	71	•		
588-022D-0020	988	AA	25	•		
588-022D-0021	1,020	AA	205	•		
588-022D-0022	1,270	A	157	•		
588-022D-0023	950	AA	187	•		
588-022D-0024	1,127	AA	167	•		
588-024D-0002	1,405	A	91			
588-024D-0003	1,520	B	149			
588-024D-0005	1,649	B	99			
588-024D-0007	1,609	B	42			
588-024D-0008	1,650	B	70			
588-024D-0010	1,737	B	21			
588-028D-0001	864	AAA	93		•	
588-028D-0004	1,785	B	130		•	
588-028D-0006	1,700	B	179			
588-028D-0009	2,189	C	81			
588-029D-0002	1,619	B	113	•		
588-030D-0005	1,815	C	217			
588-032D-0001	1,092	AA	95	•	•	•
588-032D-0002	920	AA	20	•	•	•
588-032D-0003	1,245	A	38	•	•	•
588-032D-0005	994	AA	75	•	•	•
588-032D-0006	972	AA	13	•	•	•
588-032D-0007	1,053	AA	89	•	•	•
588-032D-0008	1,106	AA	177	•	•	•
588-032D-0009	1,199	AA	181	•	•	•
588-032D-0010	1,066	AA	183	•	•	•
588-032D-0011	1,103	AA	224	•	•	•
588-032D-0012	1,231	A	58	•	•	•
588-032D-0013	1,124	AA	78	•	•	•
588-032D-0014	1,258	A	222	•	•	•
588-032D-0015	1,556	B	214	•	•	•
588-032D-0016	1,120	AA	173	•	•	•
588-032D-0017	1,700	B	96	•	•	•
588-032D-0022	1,760	B	150	•	•	•
588-032D-0030	1,516	B	178	•	•	•
588-032D-0031	1,167	A	168	•	•	•
588-032D-0032	1,574	B	160	•	•	•
588-032D-0033	1,484	A	186	•	•	•
588-032D-0034	991	AA	208	•	•	•
588-032D-0035	1,304	A	226	•	•	•
588-032D-0038	1,056	AA	225	•	•	•
588-032D-0039	1,288	A	109	•	•	•
588-032D-0040	1,480	A	247	•	•	•
588-032D-0041	1,482	A	175	•	•	•
588-032D-0042	1,468	B	250	•	•	•
588-032D-0050	840	AAA	24	•	•	•
588-032D-0051	1,442	A	192	•	•	•
588-035D-0004	1,425	A	249			
588-035D-0008	1,215	A	97			
588-035D-0030	1,124	AA	44	•		
588-035D-0051	1,491	A	14	•		
588-035D-0060	1,290	A	106	•		
588-036D-0045	1,577	B	94			
588-036D-0048	1,830	C	138			
588-037D-0002	1,816	C	93	•		
588-037D-0006	1,772	C	62	•		
588-037D-0008	1,707	C	185	•		
588-037D-0012	1,661	B	105	•		
588-037D-0018	717	AAA	80	•		
588-037D-0019	581	AAA	98	•		
588-037D-0022	1,539	B	193	•		
588-038D-0018	1,792	B	101	•		
588-038D-0035	1,562	B	39			
588-038D-0036	1,470	A	196	•		
588-038D-0037	1,434	A	56	•		
588-038D-0047	1,487	AA	74			
588-039D-0001	1,253	A	120			
588-039D-0002	1,333	A	97			
588-039D-0004	1,406	A	207			
588-039D-0005	1,474	A	157			
588-039D-0007	1,550	B	198			
588-039D-0011	1,780	B	92			
588-039D-0017	1,966	C	110			
588-040D-0001	1,833	D	10	•		
588-040D-0003	1,475	B	252	•		
588-040D-0008	1,631	B	108	•		
588-040D-0010	1,496	A	104	•		
588-040D-0013	1,304	A	193	•		
588-040D-0014	1,595	B	158	•		
588-040D-0015	1,655	B	155	•		
588-040D-0024	1,874	C	146	•		
588-040D-0026	1,393	B	136	•		
588-040D-0027	1,597	C	118	•		
588-040D-0028	828	AAA	170	•		
588-040D-0029	1,028	AA	201	•		
588-040D-0030	1,543	B	213	•		
588-041D-0004	1,195	AA	111	•		
588-041D-0006	1,189	AA	246	•		
588-043D-0008	1,496	A	145	•		
588-045D-0010	1,558	B	77	•		
588-045D-0012	976	AA	188	•		
588-045D-0013	1,085	AA	210	•		
588-045D-0014	987	AA	228	•		
588-045D-0015	977	A	71	•		
588-045D-0016	1,107	AA	189	•		
588-045D-0017	954	AA	201	•		
588-045D-0018	858	AAA	156	•		
588-045D-0019	1,134	AA	153	•		
588-047D-0002	1,167	AA	103			
588-047D-0003	1,442	A	85			
588-047D-0005	1,885	C	203			
588-048D-0001	1,865	D	195	•		
588-048D-0011	1,550	B	16	•		
588-049D-0004	1,997	C	231	•		
588-049D-0005	1,389	A	77	•		
588-049D-0007	1,118	AA	197	•		
588-049D-0009	1,673	B	241	•		
588-049D-0012	1,295	A	30	•		
588-052D-0011	1,325	A	67	•		
588-052D-0031	1,735	B	240	•		
588-052D-0032	1,765	B	223			
588-052D-0048	1,870	C	99	•	•	
588-053D-0001	1,582	B	107	•		
588-053D-0002	1,668	C	135	•		
588-053D-0030	1,657	B	116	•		
588-053D-0041	1,364	A	82	•		
588-055D-0013	930	AA	145	•	•	
588-055D-0017	1,525	B	6	•	•	
588-055D-0019	985	AA	89	•	•	
588-055D-0064	1,544	B	152	•	•	
588-055D-0067	1,472	A	204	•	•	
588-055D-0070	1,425	A	59	•	•	
588-055D-0071	1,542	B	41	•	•	
588-055D-0100	1,294	A	23	•	•	
588-058D-0003	1,020	AA	163	•		
588-058D-0004	962	AA	48	•		
588-058D-0006	1,339	A	242	•	•	
588-058D-0007	1,013	AA	66	•		
588-058D-0008	1,285	A	171	•	•	
588-058D-0009	448	AAA	107	•		
588-058D-0010	676	AAA	197	•	•	
588-058D-0011	924	AA	236	•		
588-058D-0012	1,143	AA	132	•	•	
588-058D-0013	1,073	AA	84	•		
588-058D-0014	416	AAA	199	•		
588-058D-0020	1,428	A	114	•	•	
588-058D-0029	1,000	AA	154	•	•	
588-058D-0030	990	AA	183	•	•	
588-058D-0031	990	AA	161	•		
588-058D-0032	1,879	C	43	•	•	
588-058D-0033	1,440	A	199	•		
588-058D-0043	1,277	A	159	•	•	
588-060D-0012	977	AA	176			
588-060D-0013	1,053	AA	195			
588-060D-0014	1,021	AA	200			
588-060D-0018	1,398	A	185			
588-060D-0022	1,436	A	167			
588-060D-0029	1,270	A	172			
588-060D-0030	1,455	A	22			
588-062D-0029	1,670	B	190			•
588-062D-0030	1,293	A	163			•
588-062D-0031	1,073	AA	215	•	•	•
588-062D-0033	1,286	A	181	•	•	•
588-062D-0048	1,543	B	5	•		•
588-062D-0049	1,292	A	203	•	•	•
588-062D-0051	1,578	B	220	•	•	•
588-062D-0052	1,795	B	127	•	•	•
588-062D-0059	1,588	B	182	•	•	•
588-068D-0006	1,399	A	102	•		
588-069D-0001	947	AA	149	•		
588-069D-0005	1,267	A	194	•		
588-069D-0006	1,277	A	165	•		
588-076D-0013	1,177	B	109		•	
588-076D-0017	1,123	B	212		•	
588-076D-0018	1,116	B	230		•	
588-076D-0120	1,133	A	119			
588-076D-0162	1,458	A	159			
588-078D-0004	1,425	D	111	•		
588-078D-0011	950	D	32	•		
588-078D-0013	1,175	D	50	•		
588-078D-0017	2,030	D	68	•		
588-078D-0020	1,700	D	180	•		
588-078D-0035	1,635	D	86	•		
588-078D-0042	1,280	D	133	•		
588-078D-0149	1,540	D	169			
588-080D-0001	583	AAA	147	•		•
588-080D-0002	796	AAA	232	•		•
588-080D-0003	1,235	A	143	•		•
588-080D-0004	1,154	AA	165	•		•
588-080D-0005	1,333	A	175	•		•
588-080D-0008	1,644	B	216	•		•
588-084D-0008	1,745	D	238	•		
588-084D-0016	1,492	C	164	•		
588-084D-0026	1,551	D	219	•		
588-084D-0031	1,539	D	125	•		
588-084D-0032	1,543	D	191	•		

what kind of plan package do you need?

Once you find the home plan you've been looking for, here are some suggestions on how to make your Dream Home a reality. To get started, order the type of plans that fit your particular situation.

Your Choices:

the 1-set package – We offer a 1-set plan package so you can study your home in detail. This one set is considered a study set and is marked "not for construction." It is a copyright violation to reproduce blueprints.

the minimum 5-set package – If you're ready to start the construction process, this 5-set package is the minimum number of blueprint sets you will need. It will require keeping close track of each set so they can be used by multiple subcontractors and tradespeople.

the standard 8-set package – For best results in terms of cost, schedule and quality of construction, we recommend you order eight (or more) sets of blueprints. Besides one set for yourself, additional sets of blueprints will be required by your mortgage lender, local building department, general contractor and all subcontractors working on foundation, electrical, plumbing, heating/air conditioning, carpentry work, etc.

reproducible masters – If you wish to make some minor design changes, you'll want to order reproducible masters. These drawings contain the same information as the blueprints but are printed on erasable and reproducible paper which clearly indicates your right to copy or reproduce. This will allow your builder or a local design professional to make the necessary drawing changes without the major expense of redrawing the plans. This package also allows you to print copies of the modified plans as needed. The right of building only one structure from these plans is licensed exclusively to the buyer. You may not use this design to build a second or multiple dwelling(s) without purchasing another blueprint. Each violation of the Copyright Law is punishable in a fine.

mirror reverse sets – Plans can be printed in mirror reverse. These plans are useful when the house would fit your site better if all the rooms were on the opposite side than shown. They are simply a mirror image of the original drawings causing the lettering and dimensions to read backwards. Therefore, when ordering mirror reverse drawings, you must purchase at least one set of right-reading plans. Some of our plans are offered mirror reverse right-reading. This means the plan, lettering and dimensions are flipped but read correctly. See the Home Plans Index on page 254 for availability.

other great products...

the legal kit – Avoid many legal pitfalls and build your home with confidence using the forms and contract featured in this kit. Included are request for proposal documents, various fixed price and cost plus contracts, instructions on how and when to use each form, warranty statements and more. Save time and money before you break ground on your new home or start a remodeling project. All forms are reproducible. The kit is ideal for homebuilders and contractors. **Cost: $35.00**

detail plan packages – framing, electrical and plumbing packages
Three separate packages offer homebuilders details for constructing various foundations; numerous floor, wall and roof framing techniques; simple to complex residential wiring; sump and water softener hookups; plumbing connection methods; installation of septic systems, and more. Each package includes three-dimensional illustrations and a glossary of terms. Purchase one or all three. Note: These drawings do not pertain to a specific home plan.
Cost: $20.00 each or all three for $40.00

more helpful building aids...

Your Blueprint Package contains the necessary construction information to build your home. We also offer the following products and services to save you time and money in the building process.

express delivery – Most orders are processed within 24 hours of receipt. Please allow 7-10 business days for delivery. If you need to place a rush order, please call us by 11:00 a.m. Monday-Friday CST and ask for express service (allow 1-2 business days).

technical assistance – If you have questions, please call our technical support line at 1-314-770-2228 between 8:00 a.m. and 5:00 p.m. Monday-Friday CST. Whether it involves design modifications or field assistance, our designers are extremely familiar with all of our designs and will be happy to help you. We want your home to be everything you expect it to be.

material list – Material lists are available for many of the plans in this magazine. Each list gives you the quantity, dimensions and description of the building materials necessary to construct your home. You'll get faster and more accurate bids from your contractor while saving money by paying for only the materials you need. See the Home Plans Index on page 254 for availability. Note: Material lists are not refundable. **Cost: $125.00**

how to order

For fastest service, call toll-free
1-800-367-7667
24 HOURS A DAY

Three Easy Ways To Order

1. CALL toll-free 1-800-367-7667 for credit card orders. MasterCard, Visa, Discover and American Express are accepted.

2. FAX your order to 1-314-770-2226.

3. MAIL the Order Form to:

   HDA, Inc.
   944 Anglum Road
   St. Louis, MO 63042

order form

Please send me -

PLAN NUMBER 588 - _____

PRICE CODE _____ *(see page 254)*

Specify Foundation Type *(see plan page for availability)*
- ☐ Slab   ☐ Crawl space   ☐ Pier
- ☐ Basement   ☐ Walk-out basement

☐ Reproducible Masters $ _____
☐ Eight-Set Plan Package $ _____
☐ Five-Set Plan Package $ _____
☐ One-Set Study Package *(no mirror reverse)* $ _____

Additional Plan Sets*
_____(Qty.) at $45.00 each $ _____

Mirror Reverse*
☐ Right-reading $150 one-time charge
(see index on page 254 for availability) $ _____
☐ Print in Mirror Reverse *(where right-reading is not available)*
_____(Qty.) at $15.00 each $ _____
☐ Material List* $125 *(see page 254)* $ _____
☐ Legal Kit - 002D-9991 *(see page 255)* $ _____

Detail Plan Packages: *(see page 255)*
☐ Framing   ☐ Electrical   ☐ Plumbing $ _____
(002D-9992)   (002D-9993)   (002D-9994)

SUBTOTAL $ _____
Sales Tax - MO residents add 6% $ _____
☐ Shipping / Handling *(see chart at right)* $ _____

I hereby authorize HDA, Inc. to charge this purchase to my credit card account (check one):

☐ MasterCard   ☐ VISA   ☐ DISCOVER   ☐ American Express Cards

Credit Card number _____

Expiration date _____

Signature _____

Name_____
(Please print or type)

Street Address _____
*(Please **do not** use PO Box)*

City _____

State _____ Zip _____

Daytime phone number ( ) - _____

E-mail _____

I'm a ☐ Builder/Contractor   ☐ have
       ☐ Homeowner   ☐ have not selected my
       ☐ Renter   general contractor

256   *Thank you for your order!*

---

important information to know before you order

- **Exchange Policies -** Since blueprints are printed in response to your order, we cannot honor requests for refunds. However, if for some reason you find that the plan you have purchased does not meet your requirements, you may exchange that plan for another plan in our collection within 90 days of purchase. At the time of the exchange, you will be charged a processing fee of 25% of your original plan package price, plus the difference in price between the plan packages (if applicable) and the cost to ship the new plans to you.

  Please note: Reproducible drawings can only be exchanged if the package is unopened.

- **Building Codes & Requirements -** At the time the construction drawings were prepared, every effort was made to ensure that these plans and specifications meet nationally recognized codes. Our plans conform to most national building codes. Because building codes vary from area to area, some drawing modifications and/or the assistance of a professional designer or architect may be necessary to comply with your local codes or to accommodate specific building site conditions. We advise you to consult with your local building official for information regarding codes governing your area.

Questions? Call Our Customer Service Number
1-800-367-7667

blueprint price schedule
BEST VALUE

Price Code	1-Set*	SAVE $110 5-Sets	SAVE $200 8-Sets	Reproducible Masters
AAA	$310	$380	$425	$525
AA	$410	$480	$525	$625
A	$470	$540	$585	$685
B	$530	$600	$645	$745
C	$585	$655	$700	$800
D	$635	$705	$750	$850
E	$695	$765	$810	$910
F	$750	$820	$865	$965
G	$850	$920	$965	$1065
H	$945	$1015	$1060	$1160

Plan prices are subject to change without notice.
Please note that plans and material lists are not refundable.

- **Additional Sets* -** Additional sets of the plan ordered are available for $45.00 each. Five-set, eight-set, and reproducible packages offer considerable savings.

- **Mirror Reverse Plans* -** Available for an additional $15.00 per set, these plans are simply a mirror image of the original drawings causing the dimensions and lettering to read backwards. Therefore, when ordering mirror reverse plans, you must purchase at least one set of right-reading plans. Some of our plans are offered mirror reverse right-reading. This means the plan, lettering and dimensions are flipped but read correctly. To purchase a mirror reverse right-reading set, the cost is an additional $150.00. See the Home Plans Index on page 254 for availability.

- **One-Set Study Package* -** We offer a one-set plan package so you can study your home in detail. This one set is considered a study set and is marked "not for construction." It is a copyright violation to reproduce blueprints.

*Available only within 90 days after purchase of plan package or reproducible masters of same plan.

shipping & handling charges

U.S. SHIPPING - (AK and HI - express only)	1-4 Sets	5-7 Sets	8 Sets or Reproducibles
Regular (allow 7-10 business days)	$15.00	$17.50	$25.00
Priority (allow 3-5 business days)	$25.00	$30.00	$35.00
Express* (allow 1-2 business days)	$35.00	$40.00	$45.00

CANADA SHIPPING** - (to/from) plans with suffix 032D, 062D & 80D	1-4 Sets	5-7 Sets	8 Sets or Reproducibles
Standard (allow 8-12 business days)	$35.00	$40.00	$45.00
Express* (allow 3-5 business days)	$60.00	$70.00	$80.00

Overseas Shipping/International - Call, fax, or e-mail (plans@hdainc.com) for shipping costs.

* For express delivery please call us by 11:00 a.m. Monday-Friday CST

**Orders may be subject to custom's fees and/or duties/taxes.